FRESH
DESIGNS
for
WOODWORKING

FRESH DESIGNS
for WOODWORKING

Stylish Scroll Saw Projects to Decorate Your Home

Thomas Haapapuro

FOX CHAPEL
PUBLISHING

DEDICATION

It is seldom you get the opportunity to let the people who have helped you the most in your life know how much you appreciate them in a public way. For me, I would first and foremost like to thank my father, Thomas Haapapuro Sr., for his unwavering support and guidance, for his patience with a creative son inclined to decorate his walls, clothes, cars, etc. over the years, and for not restricting these early creative expressions. I would also like to thank my uncle, Bill Haapapuro, for first showing me what woodworking tools were, how to turn trees into lumber, and for accompanying me on so many grand and foolhardy adventures. Finally, I would like to thank my lovely girlfriend, Erin L. Hubbs, for also being patient with my creative explorations, for her fantastic photography of my work over the years, and for her surprising and sustaining love. Thank you.

© 2012 by Thomas Haapapuro and Fox Chapel Publishing Company, Inc., East Petersburg, PA.

Fresh Designs for Woodworking is an original work, first published in 2012 by Fox Chapel Publishing Company, Inc. The patterns contained herein are copyrighted by the author. Readers may make copies of these patterns for personal use. The patterns themselves, however, are not to be duplicated for resale or distribution under any circumstances. Any such copying is a violation of copyright law.

ISBN 978-1-56523-537-3

Photography provided by Erin L. Hubbs.
Supplemental photography by Fox Chapel Publishing.

Library of Congress Cataloging-in-Publication Data

Haapapuro, Thomas.
 Fresh designs for woodworking / Thomas Haapapuro.
    pages cm
 Includes index.
 ISBN 978-1-56523-537-3
 1. Jig saws. 2. Woodwork--Patterns. I. Title.
 TT186.H32 2012
 745.51'3--dc23
                              2012006706

To learn more about the other great books from Fox Chapel Publishing, or to find a retailer near you, call toll-free 800-457-9112 or visit us at *www.FoxChapelPublishing.com*.

Note to Authors: We are always looking for talented authors to write new books in our area of woodworking, design, and related crafts. Please send a brief letter describing your idea to Acquisition Editor, 1970 Broad Street, East Petersburg, PA 17520.

Printed in China
First printing

ABOUT THE AUTHOR

Thomas Haapapuro is an accomplished woodworker, sculptor, and designer. Growing up in the foothills of the Appalachian Mountains, Haapapuro was exposed to the subtle beauty found in nature, a theme that can be seen throughout his work.

After graduating from The Ohio State University with a Bachelor of Science degree in Landscape Architecture, Haapapuro worked professionally for ten years designing rooftop gardens, urban courtyards, and site-specific art pieces. He has also been a woodworker for the past eight years. Using these skills, Haapapuro creates objects that distill the intricate and complex patterns of nature into clean, sophisticated, and modern forms. In addition, his artwork is made solely from salvaged trees in his local area of Charlotte, North Carolina.

Haapapuro is a contributor to *Scroll Saw Woodworking & Crafts* magazine and is represented by several galleries throughout the southeastern United States. Through his company, THaap Designs, he produces wood sculptures, bowls, boxes, jewelry, furnishings, toys, wall plaques, and concrete sculptures, fountains, and planters. To learn more, visit *www.thaapdesigns.com*.

INTRODUCTION

In addition to providing a collection of interesting patterns, I want this book to be used as a learning workbook for woodworkers of any skill level. With this book, the beginner can learn how to use the scroll saw and gain knowledge of its basic use, while more experienced scrollers can learn and master additional skills and techniques. The projects are arranged to progress from beginner to advanced with the initial projects introducing fundamental cutting techniques that are reinforced and built upon in the subsequent chapters. Additional skills and techniques are introduced and reinforced with projects that guide you through the process and emphasize the new skills. By the end of this book, you will have gained a solid understanding of the scroll saw's use and potential as a tool for creating unique and beautiful works of art.

This book is also meant to teach you how to design your own scroll saw projects. A brief description accompanies most projects, explaining how I developed the pattern for that particular piece. The final portion of the Getting Started section delves a little deeper, explaining processes, tools, and software that assist designers in developing new scroll saw patterns and techniques (see page 8).

I hope you enjoy discovering all the scroll saw has to offer.

—Thomas Haapapuro

CONTENTS

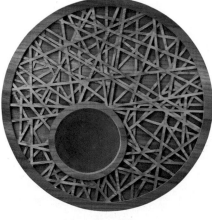

Radial Symmetry Trivet
30

Tree Forms
36

Linguine Décor
44

Farm Fields
50

Linguine Forms
58

Leaf Forms
64

Leaf Array
70

Floral Essence
75

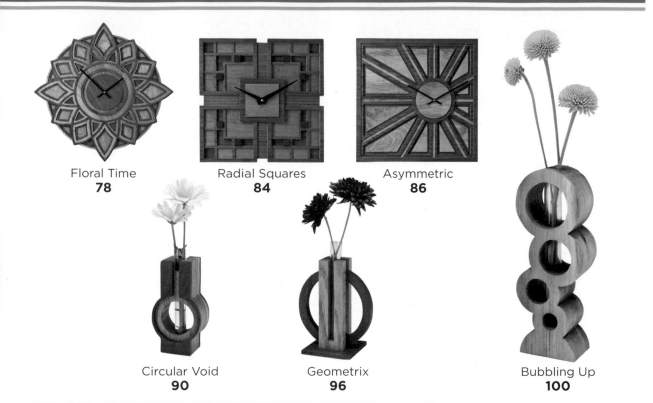

102 CHAPTER 3: ADVANCED PROJECTS & TECHNIQUES

GETTING STARTED

The purpose of this book is to teach you the essential skills and techniques you need to make any desired project, and even design your own patterns. Before you start with the projects, though, there are some things you need to know. This section covers the basics of the equipment, tools, and materials you'll use throughout the book and will prepare you to start making your own nature-inspired creations.

CHOOSING A SCROLL SAW

Choosing a scroll saw can be as daunting a task as buying any piece of woodworking equipment. The price ranges dramatically from as low as one hundred dollars to several hundred dollars. Much like buying a car, any scroll saw will get you where you are going, but the ride in the expensive models is much more comfortable than in the less expensive ones. With scroll saws, the difference in price is largely a matter of ease of use. More expensive models have features that make many tasks easier, but they are not essential to creating beautiful woodworking projects. You don't need great tools to produce great work. The most basic of scroll saws will work for all of the projects presented here. There are several books on the market that offer detailed information about different saws and provide specific information about the pros and cons of each. I will not go to such a level of detail here, but I will give a quick overview of the key items you will want in a saw.

Vibration is one of the key differences between saws. Inexpensive models are often made of steel with aluminum tables. This make the saws less expensive for the manufacturer to produce and ship, but does little to absorb their motion. Expensive models feature cast-iron bodies and steel tables. These more robust saws absorb most of the vibration, making smooth cuts easier to accomplish. (For comparison, think of trying to draw a straight line with a pencil on a piece of paper placed on top of a cheap washing machine that bounces and vibrates.)

Another item that varies from saw to saw is the *throat clearance and depth*. This is an important feature, and the bigger you can afford, the bigger you should buy. Like anything else, you will not necessarily *need* the extra clearance now, but it's better, if you can afford it, to purchase a saw with a throat clearance and depth beyond what you expect to cut currently than to have to replace the tool later on because it is too small for future projects. That said, all the projects in this book were made using a very simple saw with a throat clearance of just 3" (76mm) and a throat depth of 16" (406mm). Many of the projects in the book are fairly large, however, and in some cases I had to cut several access holes in one waste area because the throat depth was too short to allow me to swing the workpiece. Again, a smaller saw will work, but a bigger saw makes the work easier.

Blade changes are another item to consider. On a scroll saw, there are two blade clamps: one on the bottom and one on the top. The bottom clamp is only used when changing a blade, which, as most projects can be completed with only one or two different kinds of blades, doesn't happen that frequently. The top blade clamp is used much more frequently, as it is this clamp that is released to feed the blade through access holes in the workpiece. Most saws use thumbscrews to tighten the top and bottom blade clamps. Many people find using thumbscrews is a simple way to change and adjust blades. Personally, I dislike them, as it is hard for my large hands to access the screws on the bottom, and I find it difficult to tighten the clamps enough so the blades do not pull free when making cuts in thicker wood. For readers with a similar mindset, there are alternative options to thumbscrews. Many saws use a tool to tighten the bottom clamp, which can be helpful in that cramped area. Some saws use a quick clamp system on the top clamp, which really speeds up the blade release process. If your preferred saw does not come with a quick clamp, they can be purchased individually for a wide variety of saws from *www.wildwooddesigns.com*.

Variable speed is an essential item on a scroll saw. This is a feature available on most saws, so you should have no trouble finding a saw with it. When cutting fine patterns from thin stock, slowing the speed down allows you more time to trace the pattern, minimizing mistakes. When cutting thick stock or rip sawing, the ability to turn up the speed on the saw significantly shortens the time needed for this otherwise slow and plodding task.

My scroll saw

As mentioned earlier, you don't have to have great tools to make great work. I still use the first scroll saw I ever purchased almost ten years ago. It is a Delta 16" (406mm) variable-speed scroll saw, model #40-540. It has a solid cast-iron base and a machined steel table that minimizes the vibration. Its vertical blade clearance is 2⅝" (67mm) with the hold-down arm removed, allowing for taller workpieces to be cut. The bottom blade clamp is loosened with a specialty tool that is quite easy to use during full blade changes, while the top blade holder is a quick clamp mechanism.

This is the scroll saw I use, but you can select the brand or model that suits your desires or price range, as long as you remember to take into consideration the items listed previously.

Blade selection

When I first purchased my scroll saw, I went to my local woodworking store to buy blades. I was a little daunted as I stood staring at the wall filled with dozens and dozens of saw blades. As a novice, it can be difficult to determine which blades are best for the various materials you will be cutting. The variety of blades available should not overwhelm you, but rather excite you. This vast number of blades means we are capable of cutting a wide variety of materials. You can purchase blades that cut wood, nonferrous metals, and acrylics. For the beginner, and particularly for the projects in this book, you will want to use blades designed for cutting wood.

Depending upon the type of saw you own, you will need to purchase either pin-end or straight-end blades. Straight-end blades are more popular than pin-end ones, so you'll often find a larger selection of straight-end blades available at your local woodworking store. The disadvantage of pin-end blades is that regardless of the size of the blade you are using, you still have to thread the rather large pin end through the woodwork. This is not a problem for projects with large waste areas (like wall plaques) where a large access hole will not make a difference, but for most projects, a small pilot hole is essential to the construction. So while there are many types of saws available, using a saw that accepts plain-end blades will offer the most flexibility for the widest variety of projects.

The differences among wood cutting blades are largely a matter of beam strength (stiffness of the blade) and tooth arrangement. Generally, a blade with more teeth per inch (tpi) cuts slowly and produces a smooth cut. Blades with fewer teeth make faster, rougher cuts.

As mentioned previously, you can find a huge variety of scroll saw blades, but you will need only a handful for the projects in this book. The following is a list of the different blades I used to create the projects. I've provided my thoughts on the pros and cons of each blade. As you purchase and experiment with different blades, you will find the ones you prefer to work with and the ones that work best with the materials you like to cut.

Standard-tooth blade. For many years, this was the only type of blade available. It's a very straightforward blade and a good scroll saw workhorse. Unlike many of the blades that follow, the teeth on this blade all run the same direction.

- **Pros:** This blade is often thicker than others, with greater beam strength. It's able to withstand heavy tension and less likely to bulge or burn when cutting thick wood.
- **Cons:** Standard blades tend to leave fuzz on the bottom of a cut, which must be sanded off afterward.

Skip-tooth blade. Like the standard blade, the teeth on a skip-tooth blade all run in the same direction. As the name implies, however, alternating teeth from the blade have been omitted. This allows the blade to remove sawdust more easily, which keeps the blade cooler. The omitted teeth also make this a faster cutting blade than a standard-tooth blade.

- **Pros:** A skip-tooth blade has no offset in the teeth, allowing for narrower cuts. The gap in the tooth alignment clears away sawdust more efficiently than other blades, keeping the blade cool and allowing for faster cuts.
- **Cons:** Like the standard blade, the teeth of a skip-tooth blade run in the same direction, leaving fuzz on the bottom of a cut.

Reverse-tooth blade. The reverse-tooth blade has many of the same characteristics as the skip-tooth blade; however, the teeth at the bottom of the blade have been reversed (i.e., point upward). This design feature was added to minimize the fuzz and tear out associated with both the skip-tooth and standard-tooth blades.

- **Pros:** The reversed teeth at the bottom of the blade cut upward, minimizing tear out and fuzz at the bottom of the cut.
- **Cons:** Without the staggered teeth of a skip-tooth blade, these blades tend to cut more slowly.

Crown-tooth blade. On reverse-tooth blades, the reversed teeth are located only at the bottom of the blade. If you don't adjust the blade so the reverse teeth extend beyond the top of a cut on the saw's return stroke, you may encounter tear out and fuzz, especially when working with fragile materials like plywood and oak. The solution to this problem is the crown-tooth blade, which has teeth that alternate pointing upward and downward. This ensures a smooth cut at all times. Since the teeth cut on the upstroke and downstroke, the blade is also more efficient than those listed previously.

- **Pros:** A crown-tooth blade produces a smooth finish, as the teeth cut on both the upstroke and the downstroke. It is a great choice for cutting plastic, which tends to melt with too much friction and chip out when cut with standard-tooth blades.
- **Cons:** This is often a narrow blade with less beam strength. I have also found these blades to be slower than most of the others available.

Spiral blade. A spiral blade is a standard blade that has been twisted into a corkscrew shape. This means it constantly cuts on all sides, allowing you to cut out shapes without turning the workpiece. This may sound enticing, but there are some serious drawbacks to these blades. Because the blade is twisted, the width of the cut (kerf) is far wider than any of the other blades. This blade also tends to chew up the wood, leaving fuzz and tear out on both sides of the cut. You should really only use this blade when the throat of your saw will not allow you to make a cut with a different kind of blade.

- **Pros:** Very large pieces of wood can be cut on the scroll saw with this blade, as the workpiece does not need to be rotated to make the cuts.
- **Cons:** This blade produces very rough finished edges with tear out and fuzz. Also, the kerf of the cut is far wider than any other kind of blade available.

In the end, blade selection is really a personal choice. Some blades are more ideally suited for particular tasks. As you experiment and start working on projects, however, you will find you tend to rely on one kind of blade as your everyday blade.

When I stood in that woodworking store, looking at all of the blades available to me for the first time, I used a reference similar to the one I've given you to select a variety of blades: standard-tooth blades, skip-tooth blades, reverse-tooth blades, and even a set of spiral blades. The spiral blades were just as horrible as I had read, and I have not used them since then. As most of my work involves cutting thick wood, I actually rely on a few different sizes of skip-tooth blades for almost all my pieces. For some of the plywood projects where tear out was a concern, I used reverse-tooth blades for a smooth cut. I use Craftsman blades, available at Sears and other similar locations. I like these blades more than others I have tried because they are tough. Their high beam strength and stiff steel construction makes them less likely to burn, warp, or bulge in cuts. They do heat up in heavy cuts and do not clear sawdust very well. I have tried blades from other manufacturers that were designed for thick wood. These were fast blades with large hooked teeth that removed material efficiently but were very hard to control and tended to bulge in the cut far more frequently. My solution is to use the Sears blades for their durability and control and to be patient and move slowly to allow the blade to do the work. Just because I use these blades, however, does not mean you have to use them. Try several different kinds of blades from different manufacturers. Like most things in life, you can read my advice and try the blades I like, but ultimately the final decision about which blades you use will be a matter of your personal taste and preference.

OTHER TOOLS

In addition to my scroll saw, there are a handful of tools I use to make my work easier. You will also find them beneficial as you create projects.

Sharpened putty knife. This simple tool is one I rely on often. It is useful for separating re-sawn wood, pieces of wood attached with double-sided tape, and even for scraping excess spray glue from the workpiece prior to sanding. While a standard putty knife will work, adding a sharp edge to this tool makes it thinner and causes it to leave little to no damage on wood pieces when prying them apart.

To sharpen a putty knife, pick a sturdy, metal putty knife in a width to suit your preference (mine is a 3" [75mm] knife, so I can distribute the pressure of prying over a wider surface.) To sharpen the end, use a bench-top grinding stone to gently thin the blade on both sides until you reach the desired sharpness. In a pinch, you can also sharpen the knife using a belt sander, but this will decidedly shorten the life of your sanding belt.

Double-sided tape. Double-sided tape is a valuable tool for the scroll saw artist. It is indispensable when stack cutting. While there are other ways to temporarily hold wood together for stack cutting, including screwing the boards together in waste material areas or stapling or taping the ends of the boards together, double-sided tape keeps all the wood pieces together as you make your cuts. After cutting, the pieces can be gently pried apart using a sharpened putty knife as mentioned earlier. Note: Not all double-sided tapes are created equally. The stuff you can get at big box stores is generally not appropriate for woodworking. I've found the tape that works best is a paper-style tape available at most specialty woodworking stores. If your local store does not carry quality tape, you can purchase it online at Klingspor Woodworking Shop (*www.klingsporwoodworkingshop.com*).

Spray adhesive. Spray adhesive is an indispensable tool for the scroll saw artist. With it, you can attach a pattern directly to a piece of wood for cutting. If you use a temporary spray adhesive, such as that made by Duro, you can safely remove a pattern from the wood by gently pulling it off when your work is complete. Some light sanding will remove any residue left on the wood after the pattern is removed. To attach a pattern with spray adhesive, spray the pattern, not the wood. Spraying the adhesive onto the wood allows it to be absorbed into the wood's pores, which makes removing the adhesive residue more difficult. Spray the back of the pattern thoroughly, and then let it air-dry for 15–30 seconds. This allows the adhesive to set and become tacky and will make it easier to remove the pattern from the workpiece later.

THE MATERIALS

With the correct blades, a scroll saw can be used to cut a variety of materials, from plywood and hardwood to plastic, foam, and even nonferrous metals. For the projects in this book, I primarily used hardwoods and plywood and in a few cases, plastic. Following is all the information you need to know about plywood and hardwoods to make the projects.

Plywood

Plywood is the material of choice for most scroll saw users. This is due to its affordability, stability, and scroll saw-ready thickness. Plywood can be purchased in a variety of sizes and thickness; however, ¼" (6mm) plywood is used most commonly, as it is thin enough to be cut easily, is dimensionally strong (able to support itself), and is less likely to break during cutting. Thinner plywood (from ¹⁄₁₆"–⅛" [2–3mm] thick) also has its advantages, although additional care must be taken when cutting it to keep from breaking or tearing it. One-eighth inch (3mm) plywood is a good choice for inlays, as it does not add extra unnecessary depth to the work. Production scroll saw artists who stack multiple layers together to make several duplicates at once often use ¹⁄₁₆" (2mm) plywood. (This is a trick used by scroll saw artists who sell their work at craft shows to keep prices affordable and product moving.) The projects in this book use both ⅛" (3mm) and ¼" (6mm) plywood.

Stability and the variety of widths available are other advantages of plywood. Hardwood boards are typically commercially available only in 6"–10" (150–255mm) widths. This limits the use of hardwoods to smaller works. While it is possible to edge join several boards together to make a wider piece, the ¼" (6mm) thickness of the desired board would make this wider piece difficult to construct, and it would be very unstable. Therefore, for larger works like the various wall art and clock projects, plywood is the most appropriate material.

While plywood is useful for the scroll saw artist, it does have its limitations. Plywood is composed of many separate layers, with a very thin hardwood veneer layer on the top. (Depending on the kind of plywood you purchase, this veneer might be on the bottom of the wood as well.) The inner section of the plywood is usually constructed of a less expensive material than hardwood, often luan. When the workpiece is cut, its sides are a different color than its faces. For larger woodworking projects, woodworkers avoid this problem by banding the sides of the wood with a veneer of matching material. Due to the small width of the wood pieces used in scroll saw work and the complexity and number of cuts that need to be made, this is not a viable solution. Therefore, plywood is only appropriate for work where the edges are not exceedingly visible, such as inlays or stacked wall art. Where the edges are an integral part of the workpiece, as is the case with boxes and other three-dimensional projects in this book, hardwoods are a better choice.

Wood pairs

The most popular hardwood plywood used by scroll saw artisans is Baltic birch, a fine-grained, light-toned wood. Its light tone makes it an incredibly popular medium, as the color highlights the fretwork and detail of a workpiece, while a darker wood can drown out these details. This does not mean, however, that you should exclude other varieties of hardwood plywood on the scroll saw artist's stockpile. If used correctly, other varieties can provide contrast, interest, and drama to a workpiece without obscuring the details.

Plywood is available veneered in most popular native American species, including walnut, cherry, oak, ash, and hickory. These plywood varieties can be paired together in a workpiece to add depth and interest. Many of the projects in this book use this technique. North America has many beautiful woods from which to choose, but it only provides one truly dark wood: walnut. Because of this, walnut is usually present in pieces where contrast is desired. Pairing two lighter woods, such as maple and oak, is perfectly acceptable, but the intensity of the contrast between the two woods is somewhat diminished. While an oak/maple pairing does not provide much contrast, a walnut/maple pairing provides the strong contrast many woodworkers admire. That being said, wood pairings are a matter of personal preference. For example, I find oak/maple pairings too washed out, and walnut/maple pairings too extreme (it always reminds me of dominos). My

preference is a walnut/cherry pairing. Cherry has a moderate tone, neither dark nor light. It also has a warm, soft tone that naturally complements the walnut. I also favor a walnut/oak pairing, as well as walnut/hickory. For most of the plywood projects in this book, I have chosen a walnut/cherry pairing, and for most of the boxes and other projects, I have chosen a walnut/oak pairing.

Hardwoods

Hardwoods, in this case meaning solid planks of trees, are a wonderful material to use in scroll saw artwork. They can be very expensive, however, and normally are not wide enough for large artwork. For this reason, I use hardwoods primarily for projects with edges that will be highly visible, such as boxes, three-dimensional card holders, and bud vases. Unlike plywood, most hardwoods come in a ¾" (19mm) thickness. For most projects, the boards will have to be thinned down for use with the scroll saw. This process can either be done by rip cutting the boards with a band saw or table saw, or by planing them to the proper thickness.

While hardwood can be purchased from woodworking stores, it is a very expensive way to obtain material, and most stores only carry a limited number of hardwood varieties in a limited number of thicknesses. Re-sawing lumber takes additional time and effort, but the cost savings outweigh the time involved.

Re-sawing is traditionally work performed on a band saw. Because the blades are thin, the amount of wood

Re-sawing lumber can reduce the amount of money you spend on wood for projects. Re-sawing wood on the band saw is a simple process and is also relatively safe.

You can re-saw lumber using a table, but you must remember to take extra safety precautions.

converted to sawdust is minimized. It is also a fairly easy process if you make sure the saw is properly adjusted to track straight. Additionally, because the blade in a band saw moves downward into the table, pulling the workpiece down snug to the work surface, there is no risk of kickback, making re-sawing a fairly safe process.

If you do not own a band saw, it is still possible to re-saw lumber using a table saw, but there are a few considerations that need to be mentioned. The blade on a table saw is normally ⅛" (3mm) wide, much wider than the blade of a band saw. Consequently, more of the wood is converted to sawdust than if a band saw was used. Additionally, rip cutting with a table saw requires careful attention to safety. When re-sawing on a table saw, the board is on its edge on the table, with very little stability other than some vertical support provided by the fence. It is very important to use a zero-clearance insert when rip cutting with the table saw to give the wood the maximum amount of support available. If the blade wanders, there is a real risk of kickback. While important, these drawbacks need not prohibit you from using a table saw to re-saw lumber. With proper care and preparation, the table saw can be a good solution.

To use a table saw to re-saw lumber, set the blade to one-quarter the height of the board. You will make multiple passes over the blade to minimize the chance of it overheating. Re-sawn wood should be cut a little larger than the desired final thickness and then refined using a planer or drum sander. With the fence set ⅛" (3mm) wider than the desired thickness of the stock, place the wood edge down against the fence. Using a push block, slowly push the wood through the cut. Take your time sawing the first groove. Because the blade will not extend beyond the top of the wood, air circulation around the blade is significantly reduced, causing the blade to heat up. This heat can scorch the wood and damage the blade. When the first cut is complete, flip the workpiece over and proceed to make the second cut. Then, adjust the height of the blade so it is just below one-half the height of the wood to be re-sawn. This blade setting is very important—you want the wood to remain attached with a thin strip in the middle to minimize the chance of the board twisting and binding on the final cut. Once the cut has been made, you should have two pieces connected by a thin strip in between. Gently pry the pieces apart. If the wood will not separate easily, use a sharpened putty knife to gently cut the pieces apart.

Planing dimensional lumber (¾" [19mm], etc.) to size will work, but this wastes a lot of wood that could be used for other projects (especially the very thin pieces needed for the business card holders at the end of this book). Keep in mind when preparing lumber for the planer that most planers are designed for wood a minimum of 16" (406mm) long. Shorter pieces fed into the planer could kick back at worst, or severely snipe at best. For this reason, plan your work ahead of time.

Most of the hardwood projects in this book are 6" (152mm) long, so plan to cut your lumber to 16" (406mm) or more in length, plane to thickness, and cut off the extra after planing. Mark the thickness on the offcut material, and set it aside for a future project.

Another limitation of planers is that most have a stop block that prevents planing wood thinner than ¼" (6mm). There is a good reason for this, as thin wood has a great risk of shattering inside the planer, which can ruin the blades and will send very fast projectiles out of the machine. For this reason, always stand to the side of your planer, never in front of or behind it. In an ideal woodshop, a drum sander could be used to create thin wood pieces. Due to their cost, however, these machines are not a staple in most home woodshops. To bypass the stop block standard in most planers, many

Plan ahead and plane 16" (406mm)-long pieces of lumber that can later be cut to the necessary length for a project.

woodworkers use a sacrificial carrier board. This is a flat board set onto the planer bed. It extends the full length of the bed and is kept from moving forward with a cleat on the in-feed side of the table. For my sled, I use a melamine board. The medium density fiberboard (MDF) core tends to resist warping, and the melamine surface is smooth and fast, reducing friction on the workpiece. To minimize fracturing, always make sure you use freshly sharpened planer knives when cutting thin stock.

Sourcing hardwood

Woodworking can be an expensive hobby. Not only are the tools pricey, quality hardwood lumber ranges from $3 to $8 a board foot for material. There are savings out there, though, for those willing to seek them out.

Shop scraps. Every woodworking shop has a pile of scrap wood, cutoffs, and waste materials from other projects tucked away in the corner. While most of these pieces are too small for many woodworking projects, they are perfect for the scroll saw, which can turn pieces of wood too small to be used with other shop equipment into finished art.

In my shop, I have several large plastic tubs for storing scrap wood. The bins are labeled according to wood species (i.e., walnut, red oak, white oak, and sycamore) and also by estimated thickness (i.e., ¼" [6mm] and below; ¼"–½" [6–13mm]; and ½" [13mm] and above). Whenever I cut off a small piece of wood,

I toss it in the proper bin. Before starting a new scroll saw project, I look through the scrap bins to see if I can find wood the size I need rather than milling a larger board.

Furniture makers. If you think you have too many shop scraps, imagine what a full-time furniture shop or cabinetmaker generates! Often, these places have piles of high quality cutoffs that are too small for the shop's purposes but are perfect for a scroll saw artisan. The shop may be willing to give these scraps away or sell them to you for a very reasonable price. Look through your yellow pages or do an Internet search, and call around to your local shops to see if they have any scraps with which they would be willing to part. It never hurts to ask.

Classified ads. I regularly check *craigslist.org* for deals on lumber. It is not uncommon to find someone with a few pieces of wood left over from a project or a basement cleanup who is willing to sell it at a bargain price. This is also a good way to find furniture makers and cabinetmakers with extra scraps. They often advertise on Craigslist looking for someone to take extra debris off their hands.

Pallets. There is a world of native hardwood sitting at your local loading dock. The wood pallets that trucks use to deliver food and other merchandise to stores are very often made of hardwood because of the strain and stress put on the pallets during shipping. Pine and other soft woods would not hold up under heavy loads. So ask around or check the classifieds to find a few pallets. Typically, they are made of red and white oak, cherry, and ash. Often, because of the environments the pallets have been in, the wood has picked up some interesting colors that couldn't be found in normal wood. You can't tell from the surface of the pallet; most of them are gray and flaky from their constant use. But one trip through the planner or sander will reveal a world of beautiful color. Be sure to check for metal before planing.

Wood selection

Be a responsible woodworker. Shop local. Reduce, reuse, recycle, and save! Select local woods. Be green.

There are many kinds of wood available on the market today, providing more selection to woodworkers than ever before. Many exotic species are available in woodworking stores—bubinga, leopardwood, camatillo, and so forth. While some of these exotic woods might appeal to you, purchasing these species encourages cutting stands of trees from rainforests, savannahs, and other natural habitats. It also takes a significant amount of energy to transport this wood around the world. We live in a time when transporting goods across countries and continents is not only possible, it's standard. Just because we can transport goods that far, however, does not necessarily mean we should. Exotic woods are cut down and transported hundreds of miles over land and sea to our doorstep, burning massive amounts of diesel fuel, depleting our dwindling oil supply, and exhausting noxious and toxic fumes into our sky. There are strong grassroots movements across the country to shop locally for food and materials. We should consider joining this movement as woodworkers by buying and using local wood.

There are several reasons why using local wood is beneficial. First, the amount of fuel used to transport the wood is significantly reduced. One of the world's largest cargo ships uses 1 gallon (4 liters) of fuel every 28' (8.5m) or about 90 gallons (340 liters) every mile (1.6km). That means it takes 90,000 gallons (340,687 liters) of fuel to ship wood 1,000 miles (1,610km). A typical tractor-trailer truck can travel about 5–7 miles (8–10km) on a gallon (4 liters) of gas. Most locally grown and harvested trees are obtained from an area within a few miles of where they are sold. In many cases, trees can be brought to the lumberyard on a tank of gas (often much less) and can be delivered to the local store for about the same amount. Local shipping therefore saves an astronomical amount of fuel compared to intercontinental shipping.

Second, and perhaps most important, locally grown and harvested lumber is visible. When we purchase bubinga, we can't drive out to the area from which it's being harvested and see that it's being gathered responsibly. We have no way of knowing if the wood comes from clear-cut land or if the methods used to harvest the trees are affecting rivers and lakes because of soil erosion. We can't measure the impact of our demand. But locally grown and harvested wood comes from our own neighborhoods where the work is not only visible to us, it also falls under the rules and regulations of our local municipalities and governments who have been given the public mandate to protect our forests, streams, and environments. The methods used to harvest exotic trees are, for various reasons, often not regulated to prevent the use of ecologically destructive harvesting techniques.

Third, there is unique purity to pieces made using something that grows nearby. When someone looks at a box I've created from local wood, I can point out my back door and say, "The wood I used came from that kind of tree." Using local woods allows you to know your material more personally. The wood is not just a piece of material from an unknown source; it comes from a tree you know intimately—how the leaves look, what kind of fruit it makes, and what the branches look like in winter. This additional knowledge will help you look at the wood as a living, growing entity that can be cut and shaped into another form that is just as beautiful as the original.

Beyond this, using local woods gives projects an honesty. In a world where communication across oceans is instantaneous and travel to another continent takes a matter of hours, there is a diminishing sense of regionalism. Almost every place shares the same features. The fast food restaurant you visit in Maine will look exactly the same as the one you visit in California, Sweden, or China. As an artist, I don't want my work to take on this uniform blandness, and I hope you share my thought. What is something that can make Denver unique? I would argue all the woodwork done using the local Western red cedar. Maine is different because of the inclusion of white birch and sugar maple in the woodwork throughout the state. Encouraging the use of local woods is not only ecologically responsible, but also gives a sense of place to the pieces we create. In this country the best way to encourage this practice is to carefully choose what you do or don't purchase. So find woods that grow locally and purchase them rather than an exotic variety. If you need another advantage to convince you that local wood is the right choice, consider the financial benefit. Local wood is often significantly more affordable than exotic species. After all, a lot less money will be spent to harvest it and deliver it to your door.

A WORD OR TWO ABOUT FINISHING

Finishes are like ice cream—everyone has a unique preference, and there is no wrong answer. Every finish has its own unique properties. To give you an understanding of the scores of finishes available, the following outlines the advantages, disadvantages, and application techniques of three popular categories of finishes.

Film finishes. Film finishes include polyurethane, varnish, and shellac. They are typically available in two different forms: one that can be brushed onto the wood and one that can be sprayed onto the wood from an aerosol can. A film finish creates a tough skin on the wood's surface. It is easily applied, especially if you use one of the aerosol versions. Film finishes are durable and provide strong protection for the completed work. They are available in gloss and semigloss. I prefer a matte finish on my woodwork, without any distracting glare. This is my personal preference, and you might like a different look. The disadvantage of film finishes is that they do not penetrate the wood grain, so they don't fully highlight the colors and figures in the wood. Another disadvantage is that it can be difficult to get a uniform coat in all the edges and faces of complex scroll saw work, even with spray applications.

To apply: If you are using a spray aerosol version of a film finish, it is most easily applied to a workpiece raised off your worktable. Lay several layers of newspaper on the worktable. Place a series of painter's triangles on the newspaper and rest the workpiece on the points of the triangles. This will allow the spray to pass through the workpiece, giving you a better chance of covering all the edges. Doing so also keeps the workpiece from sticking to the newspaper. Apply the finish in several very thin coats. This keeps the finish from running and ensures all the edges of the workpiece will get at least a thin coat. The danger here is that the top of the workpiece may become overloaded with finish as you try to get a sufficient amount on the edges. Excess finish will turn milky when it dries.

Oil finishes. Oil finishes include linseed and Danish oils. These are penetrating finishes, which means they are absorbed directly into the wood. Unlike film finishes, oil finishes showcase the color and figure of the wood. Oil finishes are practically foolproof, as it is difficult to apply too much the workpiece. The disadvantage of oil finishes, especially when used for scroll saw work, is that they do not provide the same level of protection as film finishes. On larger workpieces, the oil finish is allowed to dry and is then buffed thoroughly with a soft cloth to build up a waxy protective film. When it comes to scroll saw work, it is not really feasible to buff the finish into all the fragile and thin areas of the workpiece. This finish is best used on scrollwork only if the finished piece will be protected from air and dust (i.e., mounted in a glass-fronted frame).

To apply: Using a bristle brush, cover the workpiece with a liberal coating of the finish, making sure to cover all the edges,

Select a finish that suits the wood you used and your taste, and apply it to your project. There are no wrong finishing choices as long as you are satisfied with the end result.

corners, and kerf lines. Leave this for about 20–30 minutes in a clean, dust-free environment. Then, using a clean, lint-free cloth, gently wipe away all the excess oil. Repeat this process several times until the finish is complete.

It can be very difficult to wipe away all the excess oil from the edges and corners of a workpiece. The solution to this is to use an air compressor fitted with an air gun (a fitting with a tube mounted on a handle with a trigger). Pressing the trigger of the gun directs air outward from the tube in a constricted and strong current. To use this technique, cover the workpiece with a thorough coat of oil as described above, and leave it for 20 to 30 minutes. Set the workpiece on a clean, lint-free cloth. Use the air gun to blow air into the corners and along the edges of the piece. The concentrated air will vaporize a lot of the oil, while the rest will puddle on the flat faces of the workpiece. Wipe up the excess oil, and blow the workpiece again

with the air gun, repeating as necessary until all excess oil has been wiped up. This trick will be especially useful in the boxes section of the book, allowing you to finish the very small inside corners that are difficult to reach with a cloth.

Hybrid finishes. The third option is a hybrid finish, such as Sam Maloof Oil/Varnish Finish. This finish is a blend of linseed oil, tung oil, and varnish, and can be blended at home. The benefit of this finish is that it combines the beauty of penetrating oil with the durability of a film finish. It can also be applied without buffing. I also prefer this finish because it produces a soft, matte coat on the wood that is not overly shiny. I used this finish for all the projects in the book.

To apply: Application of this finish is nearly identical to the application of the oil finishes as described previously. I suggest applying a single coat and then wiping away the excess after 10 minutes. The varnish tends to make the finish set up a little faster than a basic oil finish. Several coats will provide the best results with this finish.

A NOTE ABOUT THE PATTERNS

Scroll saw patterns are typically presented with the wood shown in gray and the waste area in white. You will note the patterns in this book are the reverse, with the wood shown in white and the waste area in gray (see the sample patterns below). This method of shading accommodates patterns for projects that incorporate my original stack cutting technique: subtractive stack cutting. This technique is introduced later in the book. For now, it is simply worthwhile to note that for any pattern presented here, you will cut away the shaded gray areas and not the white areas.

Scroll saw patterns typically show the wood in gray and the waste material in white, like the upper pattern. In this book, however, you will discover I have placed the wood in white and the waste material in gray, like the lower pattern. For all the projects in this book, always cut away the shaded areas and leave the white.

TRICKS OF THE TRADE

Now that you have a basic understanding to the tools and equipment you'll be using later on, here are some useful tips and tricks that will help you as you put your knowledge into practice.

Grain direction and cutting

It is generally best, when you have the option, to begin your cuts perpendicular to the grain (cross cuts). This is true of cutting with any kind of saw, and the blades are actually designed for cross cutting. Cuts made with the direction of the wood grain (rip cuts) are much more difficult to control, as the blade tends to follow the line of the grain instead of the pattern line. Rip cuts tend to be slower than cross cuts and heat the blade more, because it is running along the grain where there is a strong bond between the wood fibers. Cross cuts saw across those bonds instead of running with them. So, always try to make cross cuts.

Stabilizing lumber

One of the most important steps the woodworker must take is selecting the right lumber for a project. If you are using hardwood lumber, give special attention to the grain direction. Looking at the end of the board, you will see one of two different grain directions: parallel to the wide face of the board or perpendicular to the wide face of the board. If the grain runs parallel to the wide face of the board, it's likely the wood will cup, or arc upward. Often, this will occur immediately after the board has been planed. Planing a board not only makes it thinner, but also opens pores in

A wood board with the grain running parallel to its edge is likely to bow or cup. This is especially true of thin boards.

Quarter-sawn lumber has been cut so the grain runs perpendicular to the edge of the wood rather than parallel to it. Wood cut this way resists cupping and is perfect for scroll saw projects.

the wood's surface, which can allow it to dry unevenly and cup. Therefore, it is best to plane a board a few days before you want to begin using it to ensure it doesn't cup. Even if a board does not cup a few days after planing, seasonal changes may still cause it to cup in succeeding years.

Cupping can be a serious problem for scroll sawn work, because the wood is typically thin and more susceptible to movement. You can help prevent cupping by using quarter-sawn lumber: lumber cut from the tree perpendicular to the outside perimeter. Looking at the end of the board, the annual rings will be perpendicular to the wide edge of the board. Quarter-sawn wood is very stable, but may be hard to find. It is typically only available in oak, which is cut this way for Arts and Crafts furniture artisans. In many instances, however, you can rip narrow pieces of quarter-sawn wood out of wider planks.

If you don't have access to quarter-sawn lumber, you can essentially make plywood from your hardwoods to minimize warping and cupping. Commercial plywood is produced by spraying a thin layer of wood with thin glue. Then, another layer of wood is laid down perpendicular to the bottom layer. This process is repeated until the desired thickness is achieved, and then the whole board is compressed and allowed to dry. By placing the layers perpendicular to one another, each individual layer counteracts the movement of the layers around it. You can mimic this commercial method to produce homemade plywood.

To make plywood in the shop, rip a board into two ⅛" (3mm) or ¼" (6mm) pieces, and plane them flat. Then, apply a thin layer of glue to the bottom board, and press the second board onto the bottom one. As you glue your boards together, arrange them so the directions in which they will naturally cup are in opposition. In other words, glue them together with the top board in position to cup upward and the bottom board in position to cup downward so each board will prevent the other one from bowing. After you've glued your two boards together, place thicker boards above and below, and clamp everything together tightly. By binding two thin strips together, with the grains book-matched, the boards will cancel out each other's movements and remain flat. This trick is particularly useful for creating box lids, which are usually thin and not supported by any other pieces of thick wood.

Make your own plywood at home by gluing together two boards in such a way that each board will prevent the other from bending.

DEVELOPING PATTERNS

You will notice a strong nature-based theme in the patterns presented in this book. I have been designing patterns for more than a decade and recently compiled a large number of these and finished works into a portfolio for the first time. Seeing all my patterns and works side by side, I realized that even though the styles, shapes, and concepts of each piece are widely varied, they are all tied together with a universal thread to the natural world. Even the more geometric patterns are abstractions of elements found in nature. In retrospect, this is not surprising. Most of what we see in our everyday lives is based off patterns, forms, and mathematical ratios that naturally occur in the world around us. There is truly nothing new under the sun. When developing a majority of my patterns, I simply take a walk in the woods or through a field. In every plant, seed, and animal is an aspect of design. Often the smallest detail in a seed or plant will spark some larger idea that grows and evolves. In the end, there may not be that much similarity between the final pattern and the object that inspired it, but there is a subconscious rightness to the object because it came from something natural.

If you are interested in designing your own patterns, I recommend a book written by Richard L. Dubé called *Natural Pattern Forms*. In this book, the author gives educational examples of shapes and forms in nature and then guides the reader through the process of adapting the natural shapes into new works or patterns. As a landscape architect, I have always found this approach helpful for creating energetic spaces with an authentic feel, and it works just as well for developing woodworking patterns.

Translating an idea for a design into an actual pattern, though, is a different process altogether and can be done with whatever methods best suit your skills and preferences. Most of my patterns start with a very rough sketch that is refined using tracing paper. I place the tracing paper over the original pattern and make refinements to its shape and form. I add successive layers of tracing paper as needed and continue making revisions until the meat of the pattern is established.

At this point, I make the jump from paper to the computer. I use a computer-aided drafting program called AutoCAD to refine and finalize my designs. While this simplifies the work of drafting, it is not necessary; and if you prefer to work by hand, you can still finalize a pattern using drafting triangles, squares, and pencils. Frank Lloyd Wright, one of my favorite nature-based geometric designers, created intricate mathematical patterns long before the invention of the computer and drafting programs, so the lack of a computer does not need to impede your design development. If you are inclined to use a computer to refine

Using Google SketchUp, you can view a pattern in 3-D, giving you a glimpse of the final project before you start cutting on the scroll saw.

your patterns, however, there are several consumer-level programs available for a few hundred dollars.

One program that I find invaluable is Google SketchUp. Originally this software was for purchase only, with a price tag of about $500. After Google purchased the software from its original creators, they did the greatest thing in the world and made it free to everyone! What a boon to designers everywhere. Unlike other three-dimensional design tools, SketchUp is incredibly intuitive in its use and control. Anyone can learn to use this program in an afternoon at home. A major benefit is that SketchUp eliminates the necessity of building mock-ups of a design to see how it will look in three dimensions, as the program does this for you. You can also use it for simple drafting. To use SketchUp, simply scan a sketch onto your computer and import the image (as a JPEG) into the program. Using SketchUp's basic drafting tools, draw your pattern over your sketch. Then, with a few commands, the design comes to life in three dimensions.

For those using AutoCAD to refine their patterns, those files can be imported directly into SketchUp, eliminating the need to do any drafting in the program itself. You may have to make some adjustments in SketchUp to make the line work become editable faces, but this can usually be done pretty quickly. With the recent updates to the program, it goes even faster now.

I have used SketchUp for nearly every pattern in this book to refine the design and also to understand layering, wood thicknesses, and the process used to cut the parts. The patterns *Floral Essence*, *Floral Time*, and *Radial Squares* in particular were very difficult to understand at first. I knew how I wanted the final project to look, but understanding how to cut the pieces and in what order was tricky. Using SketchUp, I was able to see that this would have to be done by removing stacks as I went, from the bottom up. Since I could create layers of virtual wood in SketchUp, I could see what the color alternations would be in the final piece by layering different colors of wood in different ways. Without this step, I certainly would have spent countless hours and expensive materials cutting alternates and refining my patterns.

In addition to creating your own patterns, you can adapt the various projects and techniques presented in this book to create new projects. For example, the *Leaf Array* project could be made into a clock by using thicker woods and cutting a hole for the clock movement.

The world is filled with patterns everywhere we look, and often in the smallest, most unassuming objects. Take your time as you move through the world; don't just stop to smell the roses, stop to really look at the roses. By keeping alive a childlike sense of wonder and exploration, you will see that a world of patterns, shapes, and forms is all around us, waiting to be picked up and interpreted into the work that we do. Get out there, and create!

1 BEGINNER PROJECTS & TECHNIQUES

This chapter is designed to teach the beginner the basics of working with the scroll saw. Here, you will be introduced to the techniques of straight cutting, stack cutting, glass cutting, and cutting interior corners. These techniques will enable you to complete the projects in this chapter, and, as you progress, you will be able to apply what you learn now to projects later in the book. Remember that you can always adapt these projects by adding elements from other patterns in the book or other patterns that you create.

WALL ART

Learning to make basic straight cuts is the beginning for most scroll saw artisans. This fundamental skill can be used to create a great variety of projects and is the underlying technique for most of the fretwork-style patterns that are popular with scroll saw users. The following three wall art projects illustrate the important steps and methods used to create the basic fretwork-style scroll saw art. In addition to making straight cuts, you will learn how to cut interior corners. The last project will also give a brief introduction to stack cutting, which can be used not only to create identical copies of a workpiece but also to ensure the edges of three-dimensional workpieces align exactly.

Radial Symmetry Trivet

This is a perfect project to begin learning how to use the scroll saw, as it has a simple materials list, primarily uses basic straight cuts, and does not require additional woodshop tools. For your first try at this pattern, make a practice piece using inexpensive pine boards before moving on to the more durable red oak I used in this project. I designed this project as a sturdy kitchen trivet, but it can also be adapted as wall art, in which case, you can make it out of thinner wood that is easier to cut.

Although this is a beginner project, it is a little more difficult than some because it uses a thicker wood stock. The thicker wood, however, may actually be a benefit for beginners since it will take a little longer for the blade to cut away the waste material. Thin wood cuts very quickly, and the cuts can get off track fast. If cutting the thicker wood is intimidating, make the project from thinner wood. The thicker wood is recommended, though, if you intend to use the project as a trivet.

Some helpful notes

This project has a number of tight inside curves that can be easily be cut with a scroll saw, provided you use the correct blade, a simple technique, and practice a bit before you cut your project.

Even though this project requires thick wood, I would not recommend using the thick wood blades available. These blades, while fast, are difficult to control and cannot make tight inside turns. Instead, use a standard-tooth or skip-tooth blade.

These are normally thinner blades and can turn curves right in place. The skip-tooth blade will aid with sawdust removal from the kerf, keeping the blade cooler.

With the correct blade, a simple technique will allow you to make tight inside turns. When cutting toward an inside turn, cut right up to the intersection and come to a stop without any forward pressure on the wood. Let the saw make a few strokes without moving the wood at all. This will create a small area in which the blade can turn. Now, gently pull the board toward you and slowly turn the workpiece. The trick to this turn is recognizing there are no cutting teeth on the back edge of the blade. By gently pulling the workpiece toward you, you are pulling the blade teeth away from the wood, with only the back edge (the toothless edge) of the blade contacting the wood. When you have completed your turn, gently push forward to resume your cut. This turning technique will work for nearly any tight inside corner. The only time this trick does *not* work is when cutting with a very wide blade like those designed for thick wood.

TOOLS & MATERIALS

- Two 5½" x 11" x ¾" (140 x 279 x 19mm) red oak boards
- Wood glue
- Clamps
- Sandpaper: P100–P150, P220
- Spray adhesive
- Drafting triangle
- Drill and small bit
- Scrap wood
- Sharpened putty knife
- Finish of choice

DESIGN INSPIRATION

The idea for this form comes from the African violet plant, which grows low to the ground with its leaves circling around the central stem. I adapted this growth pattern into a design pattern using a leaf form copied from a cherry leaf, which has very distinct veins perfect for scroll saw work. As I developed the pattern, I had to work with all the leaf stems connecting in the center of the design. At first I left the stems in place, but the final result looked too much like a snowflake. To eliminate this effect, I inserted a simple flower in the center.

Enlarge pattern 150% for actual size.

⚠ **AN IMPORTANT SAFETY NOTE**

Please note that to produce clear photos of the processes used in these projects, some essential safety equipment was removed from the author's tools. This is especially true of photos that include a table saw. Please utilize all necessary safety equipment when working on these projects.

TIP: When using spray adhesive, spray the pattern, not the workpiece. The pores in the wood will absorb the adhesive, making it more difficult to remove the pattern at the end of the project.

1: GLUE THE BOARDS TOGETHER. Glue the long edges of the two red oak boards together using standard wood glue, such as Titebond II or any equivalent brand you prefer. Spread a thin even coat of glue on both edges and clamp the boards together. (By applying glue to both inside edges, a strong glue joint is ensured, while minimizing squeeze out.) Set the boards aside to dry for a few hours.

2: SAND THE BOARDS. When the boards have dried completely, give both sides a rough sanding to remove any excess glue and to smooth the boards.

3: ATTACH THE PATTERN. Make a copy of the pattern and enlarge it to the proper percentage. This can be done on most standard copy machines. Use a temporary spray adhesive to attach the pattern to the boards. (I use Duro's All-Purpose Spray Adhesive, but you may use any adhesive you like.) Spray the back of the pattern with a thorough coat of adhesive and let it rest for 20–30 seconds. Then, place the pattern onto the boards and rub the pattern several times to ensure a tight bond.

4: ALIGN THE SAW BLADE. Check that your blade is perpendicular to the table. I use a small drafting triangle for this purpose.

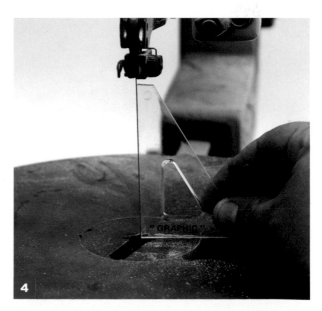

5: DRILL ACCESS HOLES FOR INTERIOR CUTS. Drill access holes in the shaded waste areas. Select a drill bit that will create a hole large enough to easily feed the scroll saw blade through, but small enough that it does not overlap the pattern lines. Place a waste board under the workpiece during drilling. This saves the work surface on the bottom of your project, and the back pressure will minimize tear out in the underside of the workpiece. I normally use pine as my backer board, not only because it is an affordable sacrificial wood, but also because of its scent. Pine is so aromatic that as soon as the drill bit has left the oak and begins cutting into the pine, you will get a strong whiff of the wood's scent, alerting you that the hole is complete. Drill all the access holes in the workpiece in this manner.

6: CUT THE OUTSIDE OF THE PATTERN. With the blade installed, cut the outer perimeter of the pattern to create the shape of the workpiece. Begin the cut at the tip of one of the leaves so the cut will not show in the final edges of the piece. Use steady, forward pressure to move forward. Do not force the blade; simply move the project as fast as the blade cuts. Forcing the blade can cause unsightly burning of the wood, bevel the cut, or break the blade. It is much better to take your time.

7: MAKE THE INTERIOR CUTS. Make all the interior cuts using the holes you drilled in Step 5 as entry points for your blade. Be careful to follow the lines, and make the tight inside corners of the leaves using the method described in the project introduction.

8: REMOVE THE PATTERN AND SAND. When the last of the cuts has been made, remove the pattern from the workpiece. Sometimes, the paper will get stuck to the wood. You can use a sharpened putty knife to remove most of this, but the rest must be taken off by sanding. When the pattern has been removed, give the workpiece a final sanding starting with 100-grit paper, progressing to 150-grit, and ending with 220-grit paper. Use a small scrap of sandpaper to remove any inside fuzz that may have been left by the scroll saw.

9: ADD FINISH. All that's left is to add finish. As mentioned before, how you finish your project depends on your personal taste and preference. I am partial to Sam Maloof Oil/Varnish Finish and used it on every project in this book. The oil component, linseed oil, brings out a deep rich color in wood, while the varnish provides a durable tough skin that protects the workpiece. If you intend to use the project as a trivet, I recommend using a polyurethane finish. It's shiny, but it is a very tough finish that will protect the piece from moisture and abrasion.

7

Tree Forms

This project demonstrates the ability of the scroll saw to cut intricate shapes into the wood.

DESIGN INSPIRATION

Photographs I took on a foggy winter day in the mountains inspired this pattern. With this design concept in mind, I walked around and took pictures of the natural outdoor scenery. Because of the fog, the background in the photos disappeared, leaving only the objects in the foreground. This focus on a single object helped me visualize the shapes I wanted to capture. That day I took dozens of pictures of different branches. When I came home, I printed the pictures and, placing a sheet of tracing paper over the images, I traced the general outline of the branches. I didn't trace every branch, but selectively left small or distracting branches off the tracing. Then, I laid another sheet of trace over the first and further developed my drawing. By the third layer, I had managed to remove most of the nonessential or distracting lines and was left with a refined pattern with smooth flowing lines. A whole series of patterns could be developed this way using different trees, branches, and other compositions to create unique branch-like patterns.

TOOLS & MATERIALS

- Four 2" x 14" x ¾" (51 x 356 x 19mm) walnut boards (frame)
- One 9" x 9" x ¼" (229 x 229 x 6mm) walnut board (to create tree shapes)
- One 9¾" x 9¾" x ¼" (248 x 248 x 6mm) cherry plywood (backer board)
- Several ¾" (19mm)-thick boards (spline jig)
- Several ⅛" (3mm)-thick walnut boards (splines)
- Miter saw
- Drafting triangle
- Table saw
- Dado blade (optional)
- Wood glue
- Rubber bands
- Scrap wood
- Newspaper
- Clamps
- Ruler and/or tape measure
- Pencil
- Table or belt sander
- Spray adhesive
- Sharpened putty knife
- Small block of wood
- Sandpaper: P-100, P-150, and P-220
- Drill or drill press
- ¾" (19mm) Forstner bit
- ⅝" (16mm) Forstner bit
- Two ¾" (19mm)-diameter washers
- Finish of choice

Enlarge pattern 140% for actual size.

2

1: CUT THE FRAME BOARDS TO SIZE. For this project, start with the sides of the frame. Cut the ¾" (19mm) walnut boards to the sizes specified in the materials list. Note: The boards will be a little longer than the final size to give you room to adjust the miters when they are cut.

2: MAKE THE MITER CUTS. Use a miter saw to make miter cuts at the end each of the boards. Set the blade angle of the saw to 45°. Double-check the angle with a drafting triangle. Cut one end of each of the boards at a 45° angle. Then, set up a stop block on the miter saw. This will ensure that all four boards are exactly the same length. Flip the boards over and cut 45° angles on the other sides.

3: TEST AND ADJUST THE JOINTS. Test the cuts by loosely assembling the frame. If there is a gap in the joints, the blade is slightly out of the correct angle. Adjust and recut as needed. Don't be afraid to make these adjustments. Since you cut the pieces for the frame sides longer than necessary, you have room to recut the angles. When the corners are airtight, cut them to the final sizes shown in the plan.

4: PREPARE THE TABLE SAW. Before assembling the frame, a rabbet that will fit the backboard of the piece needs to be made. On the table saw, insert a zero clearance blade cover. This will provide the most support to the workpiece during the cut. Because this is a very narrow cut next to the fence, it is also a good idea to install a sacrificial face on the fence. This is done so that if the blade does get too close to the fence, it will hit the sacrificial wood and not the fence.

5: CUT THE RABBET. Set the blade at a height of ⅜" (10mm). The thickness of the backboard is ¼" (6mm) and the thickness of the frame is ¾" (19mm). Therefore, set the fence so there is ½" (13mm) between the fence and the inside of the blade. Pass the frame pieces over the blade with the inside edge on the table. Cut all four pieces. Turn off the saw, and move the fence away from the blade so there is just less than ⅝" (16mm) between the fence and the inside of the blade. Cut all four pieces again. Repeat the cuts, moving the fence away from the blade ⅛" (3mm) at a time until you have a ¼" (6mm)-wide ⅜" (10mm)-deep rabbet in all four boards. This step could also be done with dado blades, making the rabbet in one pass. Since this rabbet will be hidden, square edges are not important. It's just as fast to make several passes with a standard blade as it is to change blades.

6: GLUE THE FRAME TOGETHER. To assemble the frame, apply a thin film of glue to all eight mitered ends and press them together, using strong rubber bands to clamp the pieces in place. The rubber bands will provide equal pressure on all four corners and will ensure the frame is tight and square. To make sure the piece stays flat, put the whole frame between two boards with newspaper between the workpiece and the boards to catch any excess glue. Clamp this assembly solidly together and set it aside to dry.

7: BUILD A JIG TO CUT THE SPLINE SLOTS.

Miter joints are likely to pull apart with seasonal humidity changes because the connection between the wood pieces is made at the end grain of the board, which is the weakest connection point in wood. The strongest joints are between long grains, side to side and side to face. Install a spline to reinforce the miter joints in the frame. A spline is a thin piece of wood set into a slot in the corners of the joint. This piece of wood will provide a face-to-face gluing surface inside the joint that is very strong and will prevent the end grain connections of the miter joint from pulling apart. To make a ⅛" (3mm) slot that will receive the spline, build the jig shown to the left using ¾" (19mm)-thick stock.

8: ADJUST THE TABLE SAW.

To set up the table saw to use the jig, some adjustments need to be made. The jig has ¾" (19mm)-thick legs. You want the edge of the ⅛" (3mm) spline slot to be cut in the middle of the ¾" (19mm) frame boards, or 5⁄16" (8mm) from the edge of the boards. To make this cut, the total distance from the inside of the table saw blade to the edge of the fence needs to be 1 1⁄16" (27mm). Set the blade to a height of 3 ¼" (83mm). Make a test cut first to verify your measurements.

9: CUT THE SPLINE SLOTS.

Insert the frame securely into the jig and raise the saw blade to about 3 ¼" (83mm). With the jig firmly against the fence, pass the jig over the blade. Do not drag the jig backward past the blade when the cut is complete, as this could cause kickback. Rotate the frame and cut spline slots into all four corners. You can adjust the size of the slot to suit your preference; however, make sure it is not deep enough to run into the rabbet already cut on the inside edge of the frame.

10: TRACE THE SPLINE SHAPE. Insert a ⅛" (3mm) board into a spline slot and trace the shape of the frame's corner onto the board with a pencil. Use the width of the pencil to guide the line about ⅛" (3mm) proud of, or beyond, the final size of the spline. The extra that will extend beyond the frame as a result will be sanded flush in a later step. Repeat with the remaining spline slots.

11: CUT OUT THE SPLINES. Use the scroll saw to cut out the four reinforcing spline pieces.

12: GLUE IN THE SPLINES AND SAND FLUSH. Apply glue to the top and bottom of a spline reinforcement piece and press it firmly into one of the corner slots. Secure with a tension clamp or strong rubber bands. Glue and clamp the remaining three splines in place. When the splines have dried securely, use a table or belt sander to sand them flush with the edge of the frame.

13: MEASURE, CUT, AND GLUE THE BACKER BOARD. Measure the size of the opening in the frame (including the rabbet) and cut the backer board to fit. Then, apply a thin film of glue to the rabbet in the back of the frame and press the backer board into place. Clamp tightly and set aside to dry.

14: CUT THE TREE SHAPES BOARD TO SIZE AND ATTACH THE PATTERN. With the frame complete, we can finally get down to some scroll saw work. Cut the tree shapes board to size using the measurements in the materials list. Test the fit of this piece in the face of the frame. It should fit snugly against all four sides. Remove the board and attach the pattern to the top using spray adhesive.

15: CUT OUT THE PATTERN. With the scroll saw running at a medium speed, begin to cut out the pattern from the outside, making all the perimeter cuts. All but two of the cuts in this pattern can be made from the outside. Leave the most delicate inner cuts until the end. When you make the interior cuts, you will see the pattern actually separates into two pieces.

10

15

16: REMOVE THE PATTERN AND SAND. After the cutting is complete, remove as much of the pattern from the wood as possible. Using a small piece of sandpaper, remove any fuzz that may be clinging to the sides of your cuts. Don't worry about sanding the front of the branches right now; these can be sanded once they are firmly attached to the backer board, reducing the risk of breaking them.

17: MAKE A STAMP PAD. Rather than spreading glue on each individual branch to attach the trees to the backer board, make a glue stamp pad. Cut a piece of scrap plywood to 9″ x 9″ (229 x 229mm). Squeeze a generous amount of glue onto the plywood and spread it to a thin film using a putty knife. Press the branches down onto the surface, being careful not to let them slide from side to side, which could get glue on the edges of the piece.

18: GLUE THE TREES IN PLACE. Gently lift the branches from the glue board's surface, and press them into their final position on the backer board in the frame.

19: CUT AND CLAMP THE PRESSURE BOARD. Cut a pressure board from scrap plywood to 9″ x 9″ (229 x 229mm). This board will ensure a tight bond between the branches and the backer board, even with the recess in the frame. Place the pressure board over the branches, clamp firmly together, and set the project aside to dry.

20: SAND THE BRANCHES. Once the project is dry, remove the clamps and the pressure board. Wrap a small block of wood with medium-grit sandpaper and gently sand the front of the branches, removing any remaining spray adhesive residue and saw marks. Sand through several grits, starting with P-100, going next to P-150, and finally to P-220 paper. This will give the wood a smooth, clean surface.

Attach a hanger

The last part of the process is to attach a hanger to the back of your frame. Hanger types vary, the most popular being saw-tooth hangers, which can be carefully nailed onto the back of a frame. If you plan to use a saw-tooth hanger, predrill the nail holes into the frame using a drill bit slightly smaller than the nails you will use. This will help guide the nail in smoothly, reducing the risk of the wood splitting as your work. If you choose to use this style of hanger, it's generally a good idea to use two. Using one will work, but then it becomes highly important to get the center tooth exactly in the center of the workpiece, or it might hang crooked on the wall. Using two, one on either side of the frame, eliminates this problem. While this is a popular way to hang art on a wall, I dislike saw-tooth hangers because they make the art stand out from the wall a bit, hanging down at a slight angle. For this reason, I create a shop-made hanging device for my frames using washers.

21: MARK AND DRILL THE FIRST HOLES. To make my washer hanger, mark two points on the back of your project. I generally place mine 2" (51mm) in from each side and 2" (51mm) down from the top. Install the ¾" (19mm) Forstner bit in a drill or drill press and drill a hole about ⅛" (3mm) deep at each marked point. You want the hole to be deep enough so the washer sits flush with the frame's edge.

22: DRILL THE SECOND HOLES. Insert the ⅝" (16mm) Forstner bit into the drill or drill press, center it in the previous hole, and make a second hole ¼" (6mm) deep. The smaller hole creates a void behind the washer so that a nail or screw in the wall can catch and hold on to the edge of the washer.

23: GLUE IN THE WASHERS AND SAND AS NEEDED. With the holes cut, place a small amount of glue on the back of the washers and press them firmly into place. Once the glue has dried, check for any remaining areas that need sanding. After you finish your piece, you can hang your work on the wall perfectly flat and without a downward tilt.

Finish the project

With the hanger attached and the whole work sanded, it's time to apply a finish. As mentioned in the Getting Started section, finishes are like ice cream—everyone has a favorite based on personal taste. Finish this piece to suit your preferences. To review the various finish options available, see page 22.

Linguine Décor

This project introduces lamination, a concept that will be explored further with subsequent projects. For this piece, and many of the others to follow, I have decided to use plywood. Hardwood could also be used, but due to the size of this project, it is more feasible to use plywood. I tend to use hardwoods for smaller works where the edges will be highly visible. For most wall-mounted artwork, the edge is not all that visible in the final piece. While many scroll saw artists use Baltic birch plywood, there is a wide range of varieties available, including walnut, cherry, maple, and oak—all of my domestic favorites.

DESIGN INSPIRATION

I developed this pattern using linguine noodles! To start, I drew the outline of the piece, including a circular border around the outside and one circle on the inside that would hold a mirror. Then, I set this image on a flat surface and arranged dry linguine noodles over the pattern in a pleasing manner. Using a camera held directly overhead, I took a picture of the arrangement, showing both the noodles and the border outlines underneath. I printed out the picture and used a sheet of tracing paper to refine the design, adding and trimming lines as necessary to get the final pattern.

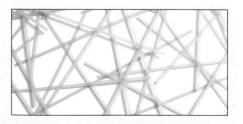

TOOLS & MATERIALS

- Two 16" x 16" x ¼" (406 x 406 x 6mm) walnut plywood boards
- Two 16" x 16" x ¼" (406 x 406 x 6mm) cherry plywood boards
- One 6" x 6" x ⅛" (152 x 152 x 3mm) mirrored silver acrylic sheet
- Double-sided tape
- Spray adhesive
- Pencil

- Sharpened putty knife
- Drill and bit
- Sandpaper
- Wood glue
- Scrap wood
- Clamps
- Finish of choice

Adding the inlay

This project includes a mirror inlaid in the interior circle of the project. Because glass mirrors come in a limited range of sizes, I typically use a sheet of silver mirrored acrylic. This looks just as attractive as a regular mirror, but it can be cut to any desired shape and size using a scroll saw. A note on cutting plastic with the scroll saw: Use a thin, fine-toothed, skip-tooth blade. The biggest obstacle when cutting plastic is friction. If the blade speed is too fast or the workpiece fed too quickly, the plastic will melt as the blade passes through it, sealing up the kerf behind the blade and locking the piece into place. It is best to set the saw to a slow speed to minimize friction. A skip-tooth blade is also helpful, as it is best at removing waste material from the kerf and allowing the kerf to stay relatively cool.

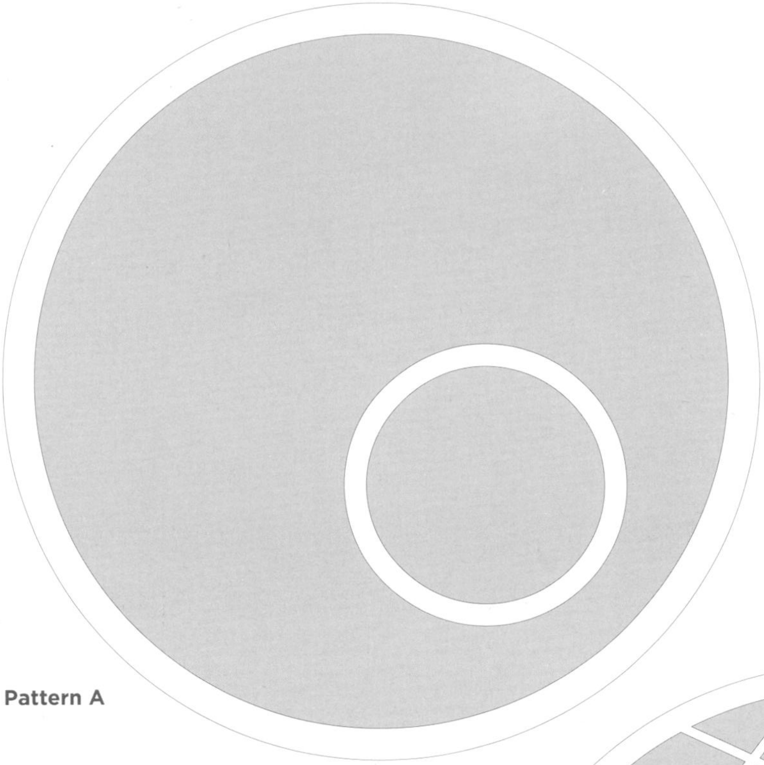

Pattern A

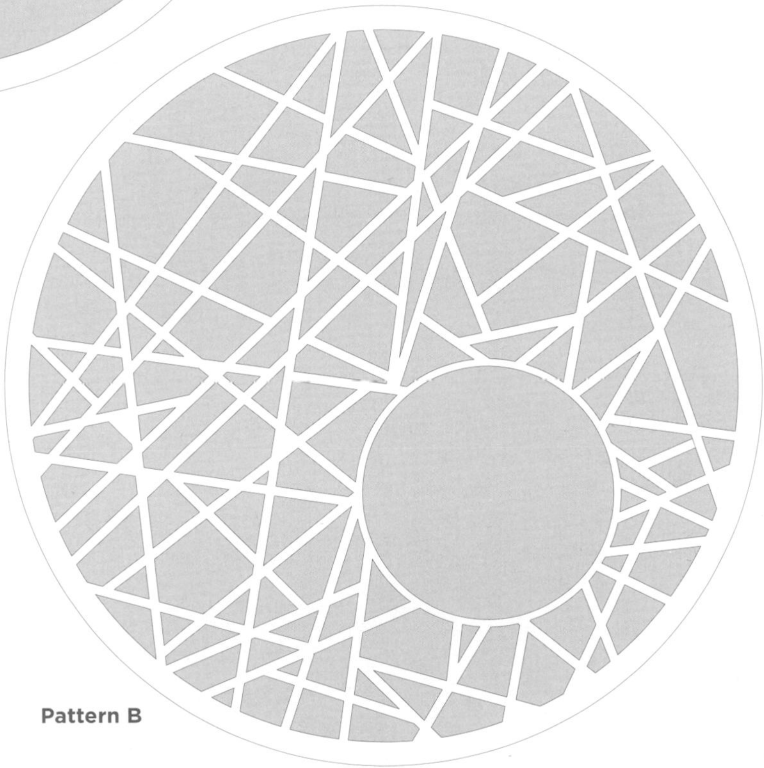

Pattern B

Enlarge patterns
400% for actual size.

Pattern C

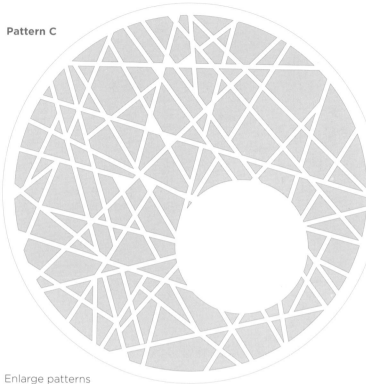

Enlarge patterns
400% for actual size.

1: PREPARE THE WOOD PIECES.

Cut all the wood pieces to the sizes specified in the materials list. Make a stack out of the wood pieces with double-sided tape between each layer, placing them in the following order from bottom to top: walnut, cherry, cherry, walnut. Attach Pattern A to the top of the stack using spray adhesive. Cut around the outer perimeter of the pattern.

2: MARK AND SEPARATE THE LAYERS.

Remove the waste wood and draw registration marks on the side of the cut piece with a pencil. Draw multiple lines as shown. You will use these markings to align the pieces during final assembly. Then, pry the layers apart using a sharpened putty knife.

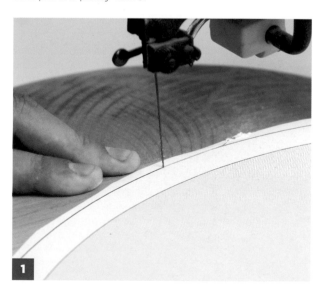

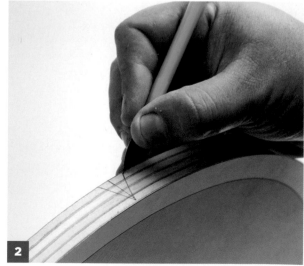

3: ATTACH PATTERN B AND C. Attach Pattern B to one of the cherry pieces and Pattern C to the other cherry piece. To help line up the patterns with the workpieces, it is helpful to cut along the outer perimeter of the patterns, removing the excess paper.

4: DRILL ACCESS HOLES AND CUT. You should now have three pieces with patterns attached: the top walnut piece with Pattern A, one cherry piece with Pattern B, and the second cherry piece with Pattern C. Drill access holes where marked in all three patterns and remove the shaded waste material. Do NOT cut the interior circle of waste material from Pattern B; it will be cut during the next step.

5: ATTACH THE ACRYLIC PIECE. To create the inlay mirror, attach the acrylic sheet to the back of the cherry piece with Pattern B attached. Place the acrylic under the waste material for the interior circle. The silver acrylic usually arrives with a thin protective plastic film over the surface. Leave this on during this step to prevent scratches.

6: DRILL AND CUT THE INLAY MATERIAL. Drill a small access hole at the edge of the waste material, drilling through both pieces. Set the blade speed to a slow pace and cut out the waste material. If the blade becomes too hot during cutting, the plastic might fuse together after the blade has passed, so move slowly as you make the cut.

7: REMOVE THE WOOD. When the interior circle has been cut free, gently pry the wood layer from the top of the plastic.

8: SAND AND FINISH EACH LAYER. Because of this project's many layers, it is best to finish each piece prior to assembly. Remove any remaining pattern pieces, sand, and finish each layer using your preferred method.

9: GLUE THE LAYERS TOGETHER. When the finish has cured, begin assembly. Spread a thin film of glue along the circular perimeter of each cherry piece and press them together in place, using the registration marks as a guide. Apply a thin film of glue on the back of the mirror and put it in place. Finish by gluing the outer walnut circular pieces into place.

10: CLAMP, DRY, AND ATTACH HANGER. Place the entire piece between two layers of plywood and clamp them firmly together. When the piece has dried, attach a hanger to the back.

6

9

PICTURE FRAMES

Picture frames are well suited to the scroll saw artist. They are generally small enough to be cut on any standard scroll saw and present a great opportunity to create engaging details on an object that can be used anywhere around the house. They also make wonderful gifts for friends and family.

This section helps reinforce the skills learned in the Wall Art section: basic straight cuts, cutting inside corners, and stack cutting. It will also introduce glass cutting.

Farm Fields

The concept for this frame is a direct outcome of the necessities of a picture frame, which dictates that the frame be made up of multiple layers: a removable backboard to mount the picture, a place to attach the glass, and enough room between the picture and the glass so the photo has room to breathe.

DESIGN INSPIRATION

Where I was raised in the Appalachian foothills of eastern Ohio, the landscape contained gently rolling hills layered against the horizon. Most of these hills were cultivated as farm fields, with lines of crops running in stripes across the slopes. This pattern is drawn from my mind's image of fields and pastures layered off into the distance.

TOOLS & MATERIALS

- Two 9½" x 7½" x ¼" (241 x 191 x 6mm) walnut plywood boards (front and back boards)
- One 9½" x 7½" x ¼" (241 x 191 x 6mm) cherry plywood board (middle layer)
- One 4¾" x 4¾" (121 x 121mm) walnut plywood board (frame stand)
- One 6½" x 4" x ⅛" (165 x 102 x 3mm) glass piece
- 4 frame clasps
- 1 hinge
- 8 small nails
- Spray adhesive
- Drill and bits
- Sandpaper
- Wood glue
- Scrap wood

- Clamps
- Clean shop cloth
- Rotary tool with cutoff wheel
- Cotton-tipped swab or toothpick
- Small hammer
- Nail punch
- Pencil
- Permanent marker as needed
- Cork-backed straightedge as needed
- 3:1 oil as needed
- Glass cutter as needed
- Clear 100% silicone
- Sharp razor blade
- Double-sided tape
- Finish of choice

Pattern A

Pattern B

Enlarge patterns 200% for actual size.

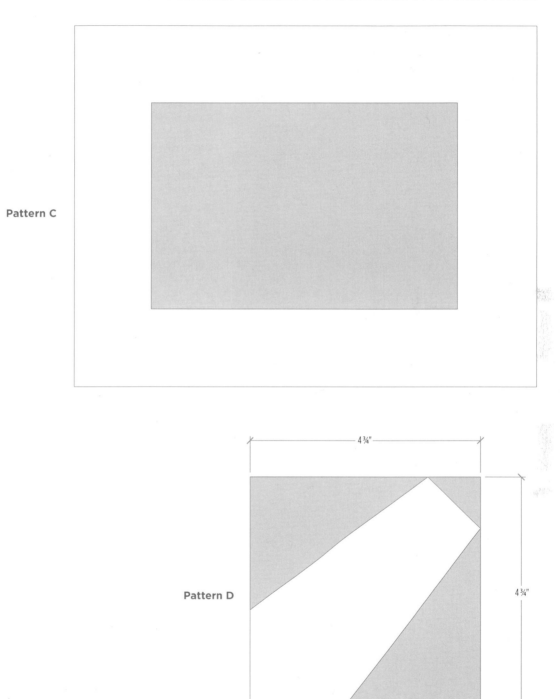

Pattern C

Pattern D

4¾"

4¾"

Enlarge patterns 200%
for actual size.

11: ATTACH THE HINGE TO THE FRAME STAND. Attach one side of the hinge to the top of the stand, aligning the top plate with the top center of the stand. Use the method from Steps 7–10 to nail the hinge to the stand.

12: MARK THE FRAME BACK. Place the finished stand on the back of the frame, hinge side down, angling down to the bottom left corner. The corner of the stand should be ¼" (6mm) from the bottom and side of the frame when lying flat. Using a pencil, mark the outline of the top of the frame stand.

13: ATTACH THE HINGE TO THE FRAME BACK. Flip the stand up perpendicular to the frame back with the hinge held flat. Center the top of the plate with the pencil line and secure the other side of the hinge to the frame with nails as before.

14: CUT THE GLASS TO SIZE. The glass can either be purchased at the specified size or can be cut to size at home using the following method. Measure the glass and use a permanent marker to indicate the areas that need to be removed. Lay a cork-backed straightedge on the glass, aligning it with the marker line. Squeeze a few drops of oil onto the blade of a glass cutter and a thin line along the cutting path. Hold the straightedge firmly against the glass and, with the glass cutter at the edge of the glass furthest away from you and against the straightedge, slowly pull the blade toward you. Keep the angle of the cutter high and use firm pressure against the blade. You should hear a faint scratching sound. Do not cut the glass more than once. Running the cutter over a scoring line already made will dull the cutter and reduce the life of the blade. Move the glass to the edge of your worktable with the scored line just off the end. Wearing protective gloves and goggles, grab the waste side of the glass firmly with one hand while holding the other side of the glass firmly against the table with your other hand. Using a quick, abrupt motion, push the waste side of the glass down. The glass should break cleanly along the scored edge. If you are left with small nubs of glass along the scored edge, take glass nibs or pliers and place them over the nub, within $\frac{1}{16}''$ (0.4mm) of the scored line. Firm up the grip, and give a short, fast push down on the nibs/pliers. The nub should come off at the score line without difficulty.

15: GLUE AND INSERT THE GLASS.
To install the glass, apply four small dots of the clear 100% silicone to the four corners of the glass. Insert the glass into the frame from behind, with the glue facing toward the front of the frame. Press through the frame until the glass rests against the walnut face at the front of the frame. Press firmly for an initial set, release, and let cure. When the silicone has cured, check to see if there was any squeeze out along the glass. If there is, it can be easily scraped off with a sharp razor blade. Clean both sides of the glass before inserting your picture.

16: INSERT A PHOTO. Attach a picture of your choice to the inside face of the rear access panel using double-sided tape. Replace the access panel, flip down the clasps to secure it, and prop out the stand.

13

15

Linguine Forms

While this project would look nice with one layer, it looks even better with multiple layers. The layers give the frame a nice sense of depth and make it distinctive. This project uses stack cutting as a technique to make the edges of two overlapping layers exactly the same. Start by cutting out the pieces to the dimensions specified in the materials list. Then, using spray adhesive, attach Pattern A to one piece of cherry plywood, Pattern B to the second piece of cherry plywood, Pattern C one of the ¼" (6mm) pieces of walnut plywood, and Pattern D to the remaining piece of ¼" (6mm) walnut plywood. Drill access holes in the waste areas of all four patterns and cut away the shaded waste material. Do NOT cut the center from Patterns A and B. Stack Pieces A and B, using masking tape to temporarily hold them together. Then, drill an access hole through both pieces and cut away the shaded waste material. Glue the layers together, gluing Piece B to Piece D, then Piece A on top of Piece B, and finally Piece C on top of Piece A. Cut and attach the frame stand, add the frame clasps, and insert the glass.

DESIGN INSPIRATION

I developed this pattern using linguine noodles, just as I did with the *Linguine Décor* project. Instead of drawing circular borders, however, I drew the outline of the picture frame, including borders around the outside of the frame and one on the inside that would go around the picture itself and hold the glass in place.

TOOLS & MATERIALS

- Two 9½" x 7½" x ¼" (241 x 191 x 6mm) walnut plywood boards (front and back layers)
- Two 9½" x 7½" x ¼" (241 x 191 x 6mm) cherry plywood boards (middle layers)
- One 4¾" x 4¾" (121 x 121mm) walnut plywood board (frame stand)
- One 6½" x 4" x ⅛" (165 x 102 x 3mm) glass piece
- 4 frame clasps
- 1 hinge
- 8 small nails
- Spray adhesive
- Drill and bits
- Sandpaper
- Masking tape
- Wood glue

- Scrap wood
- Clamps
- Clean shop cloth
- Rotary tool with cutoff wheel
- Cotton-tipped swab or toothpick
- Small hammer
- Nail punch
- Pencil
- Permanent marker as needed
- Cork-backed straightedge as needed
- 3:1 oil as needed
- Glass cutter as needed
- Clear 100% silicone
- Sharp razor blade
- Double-sided tape
- Finish of choice

Pattern A

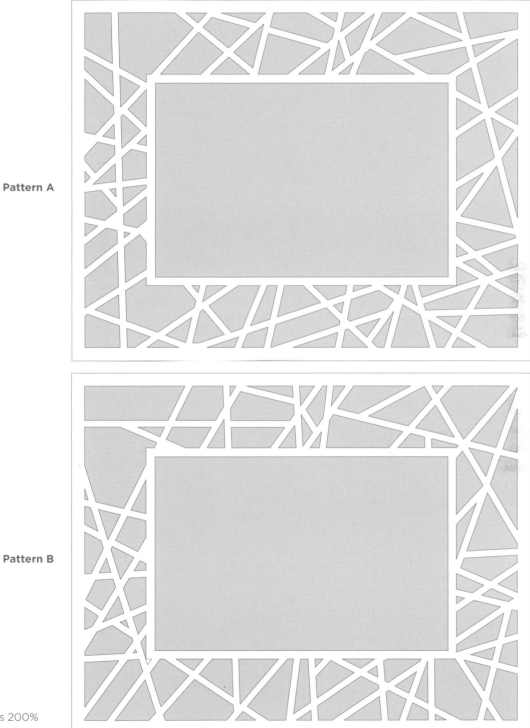

Pattern B

Enlarge patterns 200% for actual size.

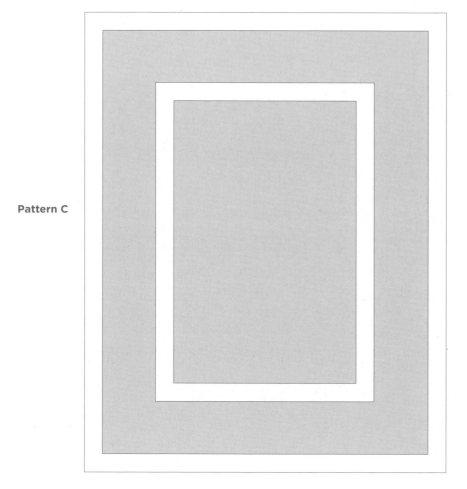

Pattern C

Enlarge patterns 200%
for actual size.

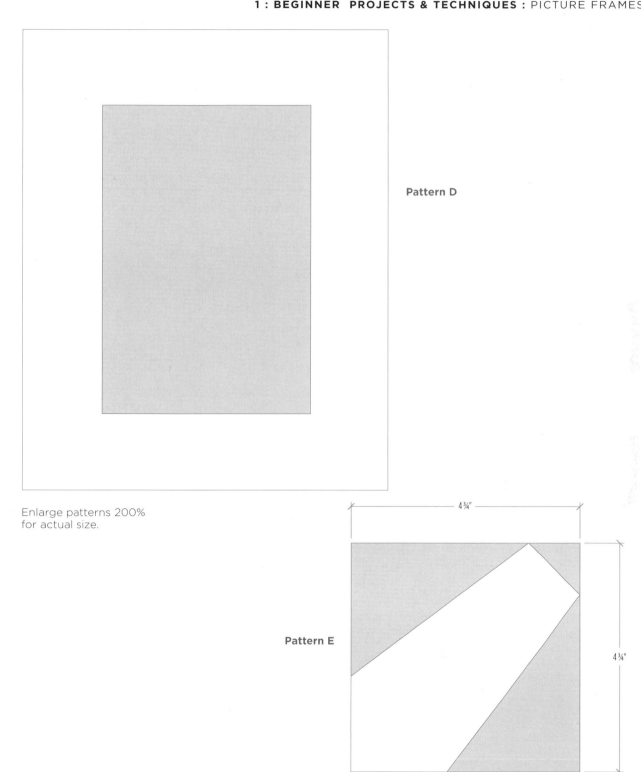

Pattern D

Enlarge patterns 200%
for actual size.

4 ¾"

Pattern E

4 ¾"

11: ATTACH THE REMAINING PLYWOOD.
Attach the remaining piece of cherry plywood to the back of the Pattern B piece using double-sided tape.

12: CUT OUT THE INLAY. Drill a small access hole through both pieces in the corner of the shaded inlay area. Cut out the inlay material.

13: REMOVE PATTERNS AND SAND. Remove the patterns from the workpieces and sand each piece smooth.

14: ASSEMBLE AND GLUE THE LAYERS.
Assemble the layers, using the registration marks drawn earlier to align the pieces. Start with the bottom cherry layer, then the middle walnut piece, the cherry inlay, and finally the remaining walnut layer. Don't forget to insert the cherry inlay, since this needs to be placed before gluing the top layer into position.

15: CLAMP, DRY, AND FINISH. Place the workpiece between two stiff boards and clamp them firmly together. When the piece has dried, finish it using your preferred method.

Floral Essence

Subtractive stack cutting, introduced in the last project, is used much more extensively in this project. Subtractive stack cutting is a process I use to create three-dimensional wall art by pairing traditional stack cutting techniques with the subtractive removal of layers from the stack after each series of cuts. The result is a complex and interesting pattern with high relief and shadow lines that is remarkably easy to make once the basic process is understood. Both this project and the next use this technique.

TOOLS & MATERIALS

- Three 16" x 16" x ¼" (406 x 406 x 6mm) walnut plywood boards
- Two 16" x 16" x ¼" (406 x 406 x 6mm) cherry plywood boards
- Double-sided tape
- Spray adhesive
- Pencil
- Sharpened putty knife
- Drill and bit
- Sandpaper
- Wood glue
- Scrap wood
- Clamps
- Finish of choice

DESIGN INSPIRATION

This pattern is based on the radial arrangement of a flower. It is meant to bring to mind the concept of a flower, that is, petal forms radially arrayed around a central point rather than a specific flower variety. This pattern started with a simple arch (petal) rotated around a central point. Each petal was allowed to overlap the one next to it. These overlapping areas created diamond shapes that were then offset to create a pattern inside a pattern, like a mosaic. An additional layer of petals was then added to give extra complexity to the design. There were so many opportunities for exploration of this form that I created dozens of variations, one of which was adapted into the clock pattern for the *Floral Time* project on page 78.

Pattern A

Pattern B

Enlarge pattern 350% for actual size.

1: CUT THE BOARDS TO SIZE, STACK, ATTACH PATTERN A, AND CUT. Cut the plywood to the sizes specified in the materials list. Stack the plywood with double-sided tape between each layer in the following order from the bottom to top: cherry, walnut, walnut, walnut. Attach Pattern A to the top of the stack with spray adhesive. Cut the project using the subtractive stack cutting method introduced in the previous project. Note that while the previous project had three layers, this one has four. So, you will cut around the perimeter of the pattern, add registration marks, remove the bottom layer, cut out the dark pattern areas, remove the bottom layer, cut the next lightest pattern shade, remove the bottom layer, and cut away the remaining shaded waste material from the top layer.

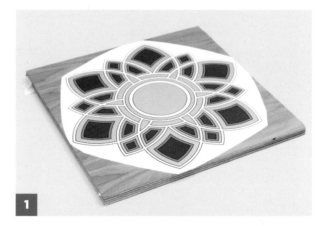

2: ALIGN AND ATTACH PATTERN B. Align and attach Pattern B to the second layer from the top in the original stack. To align the pattern with the workpiece, hold the pattern in front of a strong light source and position the workpiece between the light and the pattern. The workpiece will be silhouetted on the pattern, which can be used to align the edges.

3: ATTACH THE REMAINING PLYWOOD. Attach the uncut cherry board to the back of the Pattern B piece using double-sided tape. The cherry piece will make the inlay material that will be inserted into the walnut piece.

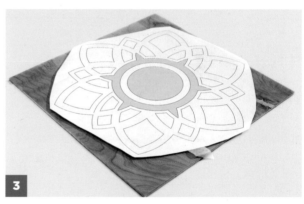

4: CUT OUT THE INLAY. Drill a small access hole through both pieces in the waste area and cut out the inlay material.

5: REMOVE PATTERNS, SAND, AND ASSEMBLE. Remove any remaining pattern paper from the layers and sand all edges smooth. Assemble the layers using wood glue, aligning the edges using the registration marks made earlier. Remember to install the inlay material in the Pattern B piece before attaching the top layer.

6: CLAMP, DRY, AND FINISH. Clamp the workpiece firmly together between two stiff boards and let dry. Finish using your preferred method.

Enlarge patterns 250% for actual size.

1: CUT THE BOARDS TO SIZE. Cut the plywood to the dimensions specified in the materials list.

2: STACK THE BOARDS AND ATTACH PATTERN A. Stack the 16" (406mm) plywood boards with double-sided tape between each layer in the following order from the bottom to top: cherry, walnut, cherry, walnut. Attach the pattern to the top of the stack using spray adhesive.

3: CUT THE OUTSIDE OF THE PATTERN. Cut the outside perimeter of the pattern.

4: CUT OUT THE CENTER. Drill an access hole in the center of the workpiece and cut away the square waste material. This void will hold the clock movement.

5: MARK THE BOARDS. Draw registration marks on the side of the stack to aid in the final assembly.

6: REMOVE THE BOTTOM LAYER. Pry off the bottom layer (cherry) of the stack using a sharpened putty knife.

7: DRILL AND CUT THE DARK PATTERN AREAS. Drill access holes in the darkest shaded sections of the pattern and cut way the waste material.

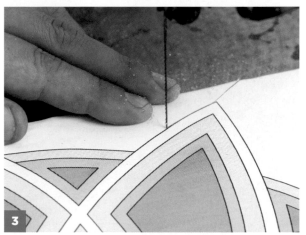

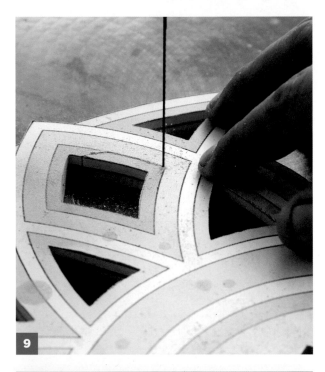

8: REMOVE THE SECOND LAYER. Pry off the bottom layer of walnut.

9: CUT THE NEXT LIGHTEST SHADE. Cut out the next lightest shaded areas from the pattern. (You removed the darkest areas during Step 7, now cut away the areas that are a shade lighter.)

10: REMOVE THE THIRD LAYER. Separate the remaining two layers.

11: CUT THE REMAINING AREAS. Cut away the remaining shaded sections of the pattern, including the outer circular ring. Cut the inside circles free, except for the innermost circle.

12: ATTACH AND CUT THE REMAINING PLYWOOD. Attach the remaining, small walnut plywood piece to the back of the workpiece with double-sided tape and cut the remaining inner circle from the pattern. Make sure you align the wood grain before cutting. The stack cut piece from below will actually be placed at the top of the stack in the finished project.

13: DRILL A HOLE FOR THE CLOCK POST. Drill an access hole for the clock post in the center of the stack cut piece from Step 12. Post sizes may vary with the manufacturer, but most are ¼" (6mm) in diameter.

14: REMOVE PATTERNS, SAND, AND ASSEMBLE. Remove any remaining pattern paper from the pieces and sand all the layers smooth. Assemble the workpiece with wood glue, aligning the edges using the registration marks. Clamp together firmly between two stiff boards and set aside to dry.

15: FINISH THE PROJECT. Finish the piece using your preferred method.

16: ADD THE CLOCK MOVEMENT. Insert the clock movement into the center void at the back of the clock. The movement is held firm with a nut that is screwed over the clock post and rests against the clock face. Tighten firmly and add the hour, minute, and sweep hands.

17: ADD A HANGER IF NEEDED. Most clock movements come equipped with a hanging mechanism integral to their housing. If this is not the case with your clock movement, make a hanger for the clock using your preferred method.

14

Radial Squares

Follow the method used in the previous project to create this clock. Start by cutting out all the pieces to the dimensions specified in the materials list. Stack the large plywood pieces with double-sided tape between each layer in the following order from the bottom to top: walnut, cherry, walnut, walnut. Attach Pattern A to the top of the stack with spray adhesive and proceed with the subtractive stack cutting process, removing layers from the bottom of the stack as you go. When you've finished cutting, assemble the layers with wood glue. Cut and glue Piece C on top of the layers over the central void. Then, cut and glue Piece B on top of Piece C. Place the D pieces as shown in the photo of the finished project. After the piece has dried, drill an access hole for the clock post. Finish the clock using your preferred method. Insert the clock movement when the finish has cured.

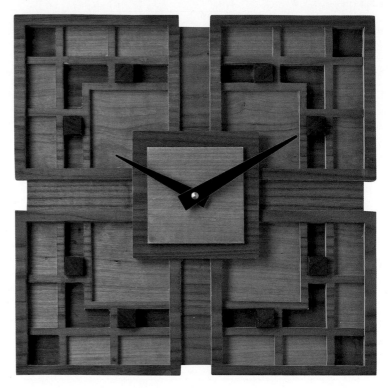

DESIGN INSPIRATION

This pattern may not have much in common with the floral pattern in the last project, but it came from the same series of explorations as the floral form. In this pattern, I changed the rounded petal shape to a square, and rotated these around the center. After a series of trials and errors overlapping squares of different sizes, I finally came up with the following pattern. This pattern, too, is constructed using the subtractive stack cutting technique.

TOOLS & MATERIALS

- Three 12" x 12" x ¼" (305 x 305 x 6mm) walnut plywood boards (Pattern A)
- One 12" x 12" x ¼" (305 x 305 x 6mm) cherry plywood boards (Pattern A)
- One 3⅛" x 3⅛" x ¼" (79 x 79 x 6mm) cherry plywood board (Piece B)
- One 4⅛" x 4⅛" x ¼" (105 x 105 x 6mm) walnut plywood board (Piece C)
- Eight ⅝" x ⅝" x ⅝" (16 x 16 x 16mm) walnut squares (D Pieces)
- 1 clock movement and accompanying post for a ¼" (6mm) clock face

- 1 set of clock hands
- Double-sided tape
- Spray adhesive
- Drill and bit
- Pencil
- Sharpened putty knife
- Sandpaper
- Wood glue
- Scrap wood
- Clamps
- Finish of choice

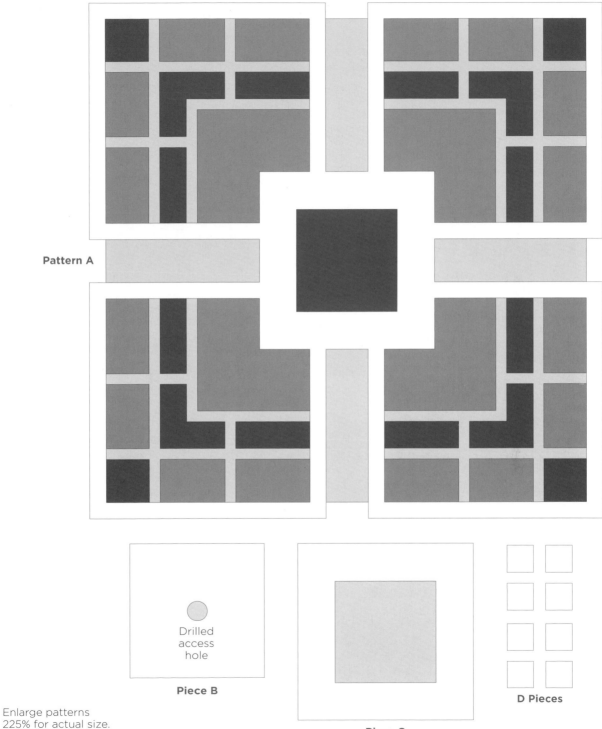

Pattern A

Drilled
access
hole

Piece B

Piece C

D Pieces

Enlarge patterns
225% for actual size.

1: CUT THE BOARDS TO SIZE. Cut the Pattern A plywood pieces to the dimensions in the materials list.

2: STACK THE BOARDS AND ATTACH THE PATTERN. Stack the plywood pieces with double-sided tape between each layer in the following order from the bottom to top: walnut, cherry, walnut, walnut. Attach the pattern to the top of the stack with spray adhesive.

3: CUT OUT THE CENTER AND MARK THE EDGES. Drill an access hole in the center of the workpiece and cut free the square waste material. Draw registration marks on the side of the remaining stack to aid in the final assembly.

4: REMOVE THE BOTTOM LAYER. Pry off the bottom layer (walnut) of the stack using a sharpened putty knife.

5: DRILL AND CUT THE DARK PATTERN AREAS. Drill an access hole in the darkest shaded portions of the pattern. Cut both sides of the shaded waste areas. Keep the cherry wood waste material to be added back into the project later. Number each piece on its back (the bottom) with the numbers on the pattern for easy reassembly later.

6: REMOVE THE SECOND LAYER AND CUT THE NEXT LIGHTEST SECTION. Remove the bottom cherry layer from the stack and cut out the next lightest shaded sections of the pattern.

7: REMOVE THE THIRD LAYER AND CUT THE OUTER SQUARE. Separate the remaining two layers. Cut the outer white square away from the shaded radial arms extending from the central circle. You should be left with the shaded arms and the white circle.

8: ATTACH THE REMAINING PLYWOOD. Attach the remaining piece of walnut plywood to the bottom of the top layer using double-sided tape.

9: CUT THE CIRCLE AND MARK THE EDGES. Cutting through both pieces, cut out the inner circle, removing the radial arms from the upper workpiece. Stack cutting the two pieces will ensure their edges will align perfectly during assembly. Before separating them, make a small registration mark on the side.

10: REMOVE PATTERN, SAND, AND ASSEMBLE. Remove any remaining pattern paper and sand all the pieces smooth. To assemble the clock, first glue the second layer from the bottom (cherry) onto the bottom layer (walnut). Gather the numbered cherry pieces from Step 5 and glue them into place according to their hour location. Use a ruler to ensure that each piece is exactly 5⁄16" (8mm) from all edges. Add the remaining layers and clamp the clock firmly between two stiff boards to dry.

11: FINISH THE PIECE. After the glue has dried, drill an access hole for the clock post. Finish the project using your preferred method. Insert the clock movement when the finish has cured.

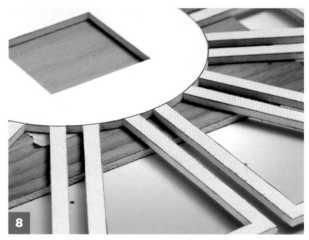

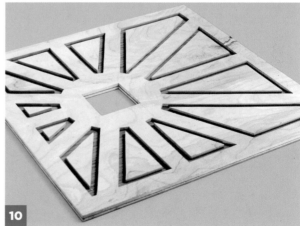

Pattern appears at actual size.

1: CUT THE BOARDS TO SIZE.

Cut the wood to the sizes specified in the materials list. If you do not have 1½" (38mm)-thick stock, you can glue together two pieces of ¾" (19mm) stock. Before you glue the pieces, arrange them in such a way that the sides of the resulting 1½" (38mm) board will have the most interesting pattern possible. Pay careful attention to the wood grain when cutting the boards to size and later when cutting and assembling the project pieces. The wood grain for all the project pieces must run in the same direction. If the wood is cut or assembled so the grain of one piece runs at right angles to the grain of another piece, the edge of the assembled vase will not remain smooth, but will develop a stair-step appearance as the wood pieces pull in opposite directions.

2: MEASURE AND MARK THE OAK BOARD.

Measure to find the exact center of the oak piece and mark it with a pencil. Drill a small access hole in the mark to guide the spade bit.

3: START DRILLING THE TEST TUBE HOLE.

The total depth of the hole for the test tube needs to be 5" (127mm). The top of the test tube should extend ¾" (19mm) above the wood. However, most spade bits are only 4" (102mm) long. The next size up is 8" (203mm) long, which can be hard to guide into a new hole. To solve this problem, I begin boring the hole using a drill press with a 4" (102mm)-long bit. When the hole is as deep as I can make it with that bit, I attach the longer spade bit to finish drilling. This can be done with a hand drill if the setup exceeds the depth of your drill press, as is the case with mine.

4: MEASURE AND FINISH DRILLING. Measure 5" (127mm) from the bottom of your long spade bit. Mark this measurement with a piece of masking tape. This will let you know when you have drilled to the desired depth. Drill the remaining depth of the hole.

5: STACK THE BOARDS AND ATTACH THE PATTERN. Attach one piece of walnut to the top and one to the bottom of the oak board using double-sided tape. Attach the pattern to the top of the stack using double-sided tape.

6: CUT THE OUTSIDE OF THE PATTERN. Using a standard-tooth or skip-tooth blade, cut the outside perimeter of the pattern, with the exception of the rectangular notch at the top of the pattern. Cutting thick wood can be a slow process on the scroll saw; however, it is important to not rush the cut. If the workpiece is fed too quickly into the saw, the blade will bow backward and create a cupped edge in the cut. Take your time and let the blade do the work.

TIP: Blades designed for thick wood are very fast, with a steeply pitched tooth that is very sharp. Such blades also tend to be wide and thin, however, making them difficult to control and unable to make inside turns well. For this reason, stick with a slower, but more stable, standard-tooth or skip-tooth blade for cutting thick wood.

7: DRILL AND CUT THE DARK PATTERN AREAS. Drill an access hole in the center of the pattern and cut away the waste material. Cut out the rectangular notch at the top of the pattern.

8: MARK THE BOARDS. Draw registration marks on the side of the stack to aid in the final assembly.

9: REMOVE THE WALNUT PIECES. Using a sharpened putty knife, gently pry off the two walnut pieces. Remove the double-sided tape.

10: CHECK THE CUTS. Using fresh double-sided tape, attach the two walnut pieces together. If you took your time and your cut was square on the perimeter of the workpiece, the two pieces should be identical. If they are not, the blade was being pushed too fast.

11: CUT THE REMAINING AREAS. Cut the remaining shaded areas from the walnut pieces. They will become very fragile as the cuts are made, so use your fingers to support the wood.

12: REMOVE PATTERN, SAND, AND ASSEMBLE. Gently pry the two walnut pieces apart. Remove any remaining pattern paper and tape. Sand the oak piece. With wood glue, assemble the vase using the registration marks as your guide. Place the assembly between two solid straight boards, and clamp together firmly.

13: FINISH THE PROJECT. When dry, sand any remaining pieces, any rough spots, and any excess glue. Finish in your preferred style.

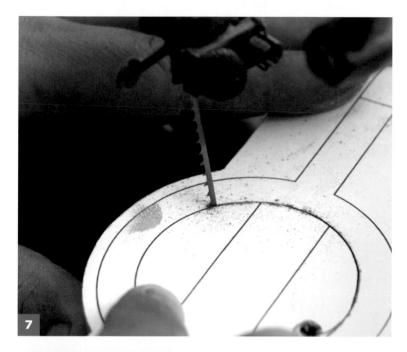

Geometrix

DESIGN INSPIRATION

This pattern is similar in form to the previous vase pattern. A few key changes in the cutting and layering process, however, yield a whole new, distinctly different vase. The following vase was designed from the pure geometric form of a circle. The design, however, could be easily modified for a wide variety of geometric and organic shapes.

TOOLS & MATERIALS LIST

- One 5⅜" x 5" x ½" (137 x 127 x 13mm) walnut board
- Two 5⅜" x 1½" x ½" (137 x 38 x 13mm) oak boards
- One 3" x 3" x ¼" (76 x 76 x 6mm) walnut board
- One 20 x 150mm test tube
- Spray adhesive
- Drill press or drill and bit
- Sandpaper
- Wood glue
- Scrap wood
- Clamps
- Pencil
- One ¾" (19mm) spade wood boring bit, 4" (102mm) long
- One ¾" (19mm) spade wood boring bit, 6" (152mm) long or longer
- Masking tape
- Finish of choice

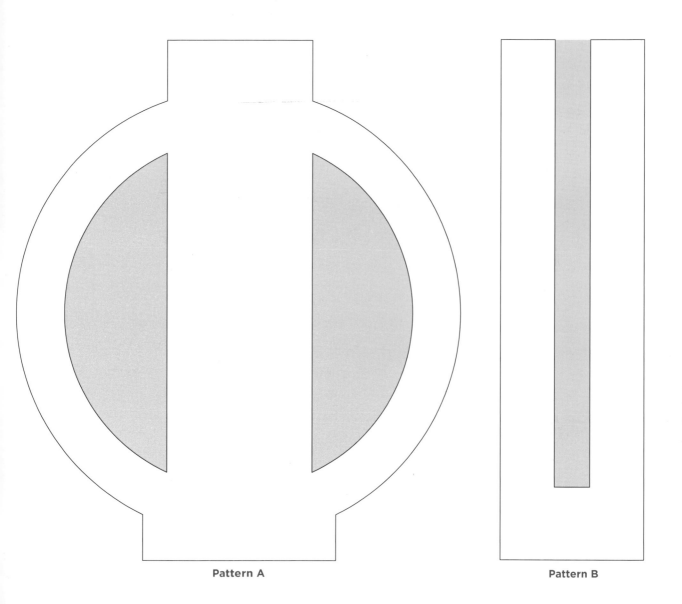

Pattern A

Pattern B

Patterns appear at actual size.

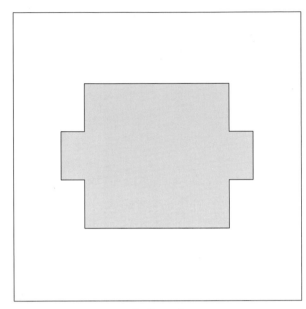

Pattern C

Pattern appears at actual size.

1: CUT THE BOARDS TO SIZE. Cut the wood to the sizes specified in the materials list, making sure to cut all the pieces so that the wood grain is running in the same direction. Pay careful attention to the wood grain when cutting the boards to size and later when cutting and assembling the project pieces. The wood grain for all the project pieces must run in the same direction. If the wood is cut or assembled so the grain of one piece runs at right angles to the grain of another piece, the edge of the assembled vase will not remain smooth, but will develop a stair-step appearance as the wood pieces pull in opposite directions.

2: ATTACH THE PATTERNS. Attach Pattern A to the larger walnut piece and Pattern C to the smaller walnut piece using spray adhesive. Attach Pattern B to one of the oak pieces.

3: DRILL AND CUT PIECE A. Drill an access hole into the shaded waste material of the larger walnut piece with Pattern A attached. When cutting in the center along the spine, cut a little to the inside of the line. This line will be cut flush during a later step.

4: DRILL AND CUT PIECE C. Drill an access hole into the shaded waste material of the smaller walnut piece with Pattern C attached and cut away the waste material.

5: SAND PIECES A AND C. Remove the patterns from Pieces A and C and sand.

6: ATTACH THE OAK PIECES. Apply a small film of glue to the oak pieces and attach one on each side of the center spine of Piece A. Make sure the piece with Pattern B attached is facing outward so you can see the pattern. Place the project between two sturdy boards and clamp firmly together. Allow to dry.

7: MARK THE CENTER POINT AND DRILL. When the piece has dried, mark the center point at the top end of Piece A. Drill a hole to receive the test tube, using the process described in the *Circular Void* project (page 90).

8: CUT THE SPINE FLUSH. Lay the piece on its side, insert the blade into one of the spaces on either side of the spine, and tighten the blade. Starting at the inside corner, remove any portion of the middle walnut piece (Piece A) that extends beyond the face of the oak pieces above and below. Use the oak pieces to guide the saw blade, without cutting the oak pieces themselves. Repeat on the other side of the spine.

9: DRILL AND CUT PATTERN B. Cut the waste area from Pattern B. Since most of the wood in this area has been drilled out previously, this cut should be fairly fast. Remove the pattern and sand.

10: FIT AND GLUE PIECE C. Piece C acts as the base and should fit around the inside spine of the project. Test the fit of Piece C. It should fit snugly around the spine, but not too tightly. If the hole in Piece C is a little too small, set the base of the workpiece over the hole in Piece C and trace the outline with a pencil. Recut the hole just shy of the pencil line and check the fit again. Repeat this step as necessary to achieve a snug, even fit. Then, apply a small amount of glue to the inside edges of the hole in Piece C and insert the base of the vase.

11: FINISH THE PIECE. When the glue has dried, give any rough areas a final sanding. To sand the test tube access hole, wrap a piece of sandpaper over a dowel rod and use it to sand the interior of the hole. Finish the piece using your preferred method.

9

Bubbling Up

This project is thick wood cutting in its simplest form; however, it also demonstrates that a simple design and basic cuts can produce a very fine project. Use the techniques previously introduced in this section to cut and assemble the vase.

DESIGN INSPIRATION

This bud vase, as its name implies, was inspired by air bubbles floating through the water toward the surface. The bubbles start small at the base, and grow larger as they reach the top, further implying movement upward. The idea of bubbles and water in the form seemed fitting inspirations for a bud vase.

TOOLS & MATERIALS

- One 2¾" x 7" x 1½" (70 x 178 x 38mm) walnut board (Note: For this project, I used a highly colored piece of walnut to give further interest to this simple bud vase. You can elect to use a single piece of wood of this thickness, or experiment with layers of different colored woods glued together to create the wood blank.)

- One 20 x 150mm test tube

- Spray adhesive

- Drill press or drill and bit

- Sandpaper

- Pencil

- One ¾" (19mm) spade wood boring bit, 4" (102mm) long

- One ¾" (19mm) spade wood boring bit, 6" (152mm) long or longer

- Masking tape

- Finish of choice

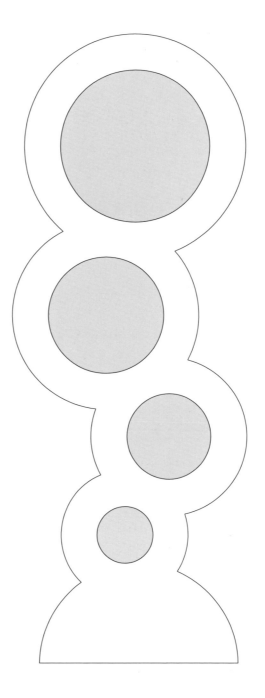

Pattern appears at actual size.

Tips on wood grain and box construction

While the scroll saw can be used to make unique boxes, creating boxes takes special consideration. Unlike the rest of the projects in this book, boxes are susceptible to seasonal movement of the wood. If not planned for, this can turn a beautiful box into an ill fitting and distorted piece in a few months.

Seasonal movement, in this case, refers to the expansion and contraction of wood based on the seasons. Since wood is an organic material made of strands of tissues running parallel to each other (wood grain), it is far less static than stone, plastic, or other inert materials. In the hot, humid summer, wood tends to expand as ambient moisture and heat are drawn into the wood. In the winter, wood tends to shrink as ambient moisture and temperature decrease. Finish retards wood's natural pattern of expansion and contraction by filling its pores with a film that slows the absorption and release of moisture from the wood's tissues. Some finishes do a better job of this than others; however, no finish completely deters moisture exchange, and all wood objects must be designed to accommodate the movement.

Plywood is less susceptible to seasonal movement, as it is made of several layers of wood stacked perpendicular to one another and glued securely to restrict movement. With solid pieces of wood like the hardwoods used for the box projects, however, seasonal movement is inevitable, especially because the wood pieces will be very thin.

Since we cannot prevent seasonal movement in projects, we must plan for it. For all of the boxes that follow, layers of dimensional lumber are stacked and glued together to make a box blank. Mimicking the construction of plywood and stacking the layers of the wood blank perpendicular to one another will not provide stability against seasonal movement, as there are too few layers. If stacked perpendicular to one another, the boards will actually tend to work against each other, pushing and pulling at right angles, which can lead to cupped and warped projects. Because of this, it is better to align all the layers of the wood blank parallel to one another. The pieces can then contract and expand in the same direction and will be less likely to separate. Some warping may still occur, but this will settle out again during the next season.

As mentioned previously in the book, you can add extra stability to a project by using quarter-sawn wood. You might also try creating your own version of plywood by rip cutting a piece of wood into two thin boards, book matching the boards, and then gluing them back together as described on page 25.

Arabian

DESIGN INSPIRATION

Islam prohibits the incorporation and representation of living forms in religious artwork, believing that God is solely responsible for the creation of living things and that mimicking those forms is presumptuous and sacrilegious. Consequently, cultures in which Islam is the predominant religion have spent hundreds of years exploring geometric forms, patterns, and relationships. Many of these forms are perfectly adaptable to boxes made with the scroll saw. The basis of this box came from an image I found on the Internet of a large ceiling fresco with tessellated interweaving forms. Tucked into the image were little snowflake-like shapes—a radial arrangement of interconnected petals. To develop a woodworking pattern based on this

snowflake shape, I first traced the original form. Then, I adjusted the number of arms and their shape, the way the arms overlapped, and the offsets of the resulting shapes. This process yielded dozens of variations, each distinctly different from the original but bearing subtle references to the first snowflake form.

TOOLS & MATERIALS

- Three 5¾" x 5½" x ¼" (146 x 140 x 6mm) walnut boards
- Two 5¾" x 5½" x ½" (146 x 140 x 13mm) oak boards
- Wood glue
- Clamps
- Double-sided tape
- Spray adhesive
- Pencil
- Sharpened putty knife
- Drill and bit
- Band saw
- Sandpaper
- Radial orbit sander (optional)
- Table belt sander (optional)
- Scrap wood
- Wood putty (optional)
- Newspaper (optional)
- Finish of choice

Pattern A

Pattern appears at actual size.

Pattern B

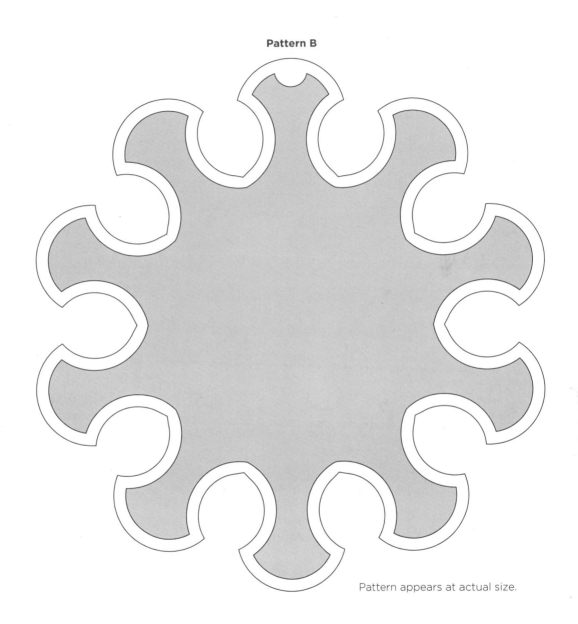

Pattern appears at actual size.

1: CHECK YOUR SCROLL SAW. Before cutting the materials from the materials list, check the maximum height you can cut on your scroll saw. If you have a hold-down clamp installed, remove it. The final height of this box will be 1¼" (32mm). If your saw cannot cut wood this thick, reduce the thickness of the oak boards used for the main box body. Once you've checked your saw, cut the boards to the sizes shown on the materials list. Pay careful attention to the wood grain when cutting the boards to size, when assembling the box blank, and when cutting and assembling the project pieces. As mentioned on page 104, make sure you assemble the box so the grain of all the layers runs parallel.

2: MAKE THE BLANK. To make the box blank, begin by gluing a walnut board between the two oak boards. Clamp together firmly and allow to dry.

3: ADD THE WALNUT PIECES. Remove the blank from the clamps. Using double-sided tape, attach the remaining pieces of walnut, one to the bottom and one to the top of the blank. Clamp the blank together again and let it sit for about five minutes, giving the tape time to develop a strong bond with the wood pieces.

4: ATTACH PATTERN A. Remove the blank from the clamps. Make a copy of Pattern A and attach it to the top of the blank using spray adhesive.

5: CUT THE OUTSIDE OF THE PATTERN.

Using a straight blade or skip-tooth blade designed for wood chip removal, begin to cut the outside perimeter of the pattern. If your saw has a variable speed setting, set it to a medium/high speed. Cutting wood of this thickness can be time consuming, but be patient and let the blade do the work. If you push the workpiece too hard into the blade, then the blade may bow backward, causing an uneven, cupped edge in the side of the box. When you come to the inside corners of the pattern, it is a good idea to let the blade idle in place for a few seconds. Often the blade will bow somewhat in these thicker cuts, usually with the bottom of the blade behind the top, normally about ⅟₁₆" (2mm). Idling the blade in place before changing direction gives the bottom of the blade a chance to catch up, so the blade will pull straight.

6: MARK THE SIDES. Draw registration marks on the side of the box with a pencil to aid in the final assembly.

7: REMOVE THE OUTER WALNUT PIECES. Using a sharpened putty knife, gently pry the top and bottom walnut pieces off the center portion of the blank. Remove any remaining pieces of double-sided tape from the wood.

8: ATTACH PATTERN B. To create the void in the box, attach Pattern B to the blank using spray adhesive. To align the pattern with the outside edge of the box, either cut the outside edge of the pattern with a pair of scissors and line up the edge of the pattern with the edge of the box, or hold up the box to a strong light source so that the box is silhouetted against the pattern. When the pattern is in place, rub the paper swiftly and firmly with your hand to ensure a good bond.

9: DRILL AND CUT PATTERN B. Drill an access hole at the edge of the waste material. Feed the blade into the hole and begin the cut. The same rules used for cutting the outside of the box apply here, but are even more important than before. If the blade bulges on the inside cut, then the waste material may be very difficult or even impossible to remove in one piece. Take your time and let the blade do the work. When the inside waste material has been cut free, remove it and set it aside to make the lid catch later.

5

TIP: The woods used for this project (oak and walnut) are not inclined to burn during a heavy cut, but using a skip-tooth blade will help keep your blade cool while cutting, because the missing teeth let sawdust leave the cut easily. If you do smell the wood burning during a heavy cut, then slow the speed of the blade a bit. You can add clear plastic tape to the bottom of the workpiece to provide lubrication in the cuts, which helps reduce burning. This is not a necessary step unless you are working with woods prone to burning, like cherry.

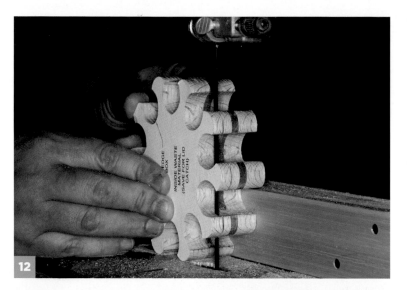

10: DRILL AND CUT PATTERN A.
One of the walnut pieces you removed during Step 7 should still have Pattern A attached to it. Drill access holes into the waste areas and use a narrow blade to cut away the waste material. A narrow blade will help make the tight inside corner cuts.

11: MARK THE LID CATCH.
The inner waste material removed during Step 9 will be used to make the lid catch. Make a mark on the side of the wood ¼" (6mm) down from the top of the piece. Flip the piece on its side and set the band saw fence to align the blade with this mark.

12: CUT THE LID CATCH.
Cut the ¼" (6mm) slab from the top of the piece. Hold the wood firmly and pay close attention to your fingers at all times. Band saws can be very dangerous, particularly when cutting short, irregularly shaped objects.

13: REMOVE THE PATTERN AND SAND.
When the slab has been cut free, remove the pattern and sand the top and bottom flat. If you own a table belt sander, it will speed the sanding process significantly.

14: SAND THE ENTIRE BOX.
Remove any remaining pattern paper and sand all pieces of the box. To minimize rounding the edges, lay a sheet of sandpaper down on a flat surface and drag the pieces back and forth over the paper in the direction of the wood grain.

15: APPLY GLUE TO THE LID.
To assemble the lid, place Piece A (the walnut piece cut during Step 10) upside down on the table. Apply small drops of glue to the wood and smear it to a thin coat using a finger or disposable brush. Keep the glue ⅛" (3mm) from the edge of the lid. This portion of the lid will be visible beyond the lid catch.

16: ATTACH THE LID CATCH. Place the body of the box on top of the lid, aligning it using the registration marks made earlier. Carefully, push the lid catch through the box body until it touches the bottom of the lid. Apply steady, even pressure on the lid catch for about 30 seconds to let an initial bond in the glue set. Then, still holding the lid catch down with your fingers, gently lift the box body off the lid.

17: CLAMP THE LID. Place the lid between two stout, flat boards and clamp firmly together.

18: GLUE THE BOTTOM. To finish assembly, apply a small film of glue to the bottom of the box body and press the remaining walnut piece into place, aligning it with the registration marks. Set this piece between two boards and clamp firmly together.

19: TEST THE FIT. When the pieces are dry, test the fit. If there are any rough areas or places where the glue has squeezed out, gently sand them until smooth.

20: FINISH THE PIECE. Finish the box using your preferred method.

15

16

17

Alternative inlay lid

You can change the design of this box by creating an inlaid lid instead of using the raised walnut piece as shown previously. Using inlay is a simple way to create a different box with its own unique charm while still using the same pattern. To create the inlaid lid, you will need an additional 5 ¾" x 5 ½" x ¼" (146 x 140 x 6mm) oak board. Follow Steps 1–7 listed previously, and then follow the following directions.

Pattern appears at actual size.

1: TAPE THE LAYERS. Using double-sided tape, attach Piece A (the walnut piece with Pattern A attached) to the 5¾" x 5½" x ¼" (146 x 140 x 6mm) oak board, making sure both pieces have been planed to the same thickness.

2: DRILL THE ACCESS HOLES. Use a small drill bit to drill holes just large enough for a thin blade to pass through. Drill the holes in the corner of waste material and through both pieces of wood.

3: CUT OUT THE PATTERN. Carefully cut out the inlay material, following the pattern.

4: MARK THE INLAY PIECES. The pattern is numbered to help you keep track of where the inlay pieces go. After making each cut, use a pencil to mark the bottom of each oak piece with the number of the cut. Discard the walnut pieces and the oak board.

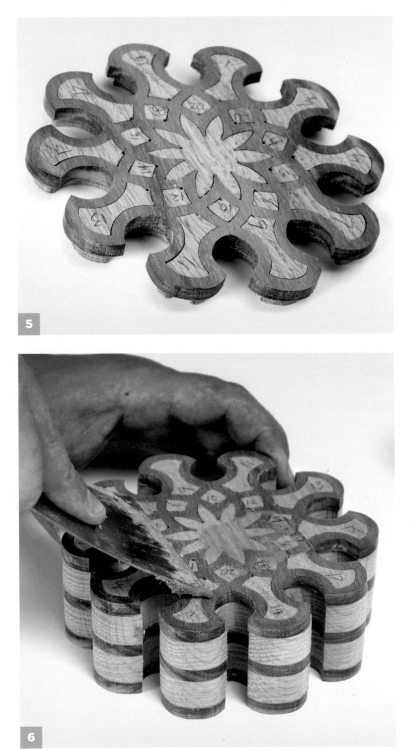

5: GLUE THE INLAY PIECES. Apply a small film of glue to the edges of the oak inlay pieces and reassemble the lid, matching the numbers on the inlay pieces with the numbers on the pattern. Clamp the lid firmly between two sturdy flat boards with newspaper between the boards and the workpiece. When the piece has dried, remove any remaining pattern paper.

6: FILL WITH PUTTY. Use a putty knife to fill the gaps around the inlay pieces caused by the kerfs and the access holes with oak wood putty.

7: SAND THE LID. When the putty has dried, sand away any excess and give both sides a final sanding.

8: FINISH THE PROJECT. Use the steps described previously to cut and attach the lid catch to the bottom of the lid and to finish the box assembly. Check the fit, sand, and finish using your preferred method.

Elliptical Array

This project can be made using the same process employed for the *Arabian* box (page 105) and has an inlaid lid. Make sure you pay particular attention to the wood grain of the pieces used to make the box. Cut all the boards so the wood grain is running in the same direction, and align the grain of all the pieces before cutting and assembling the box.

TOOLS & MATERIALS

- Three 5½"x 5½" x ¼" (140 x 140 x 6mm) walnut boards
- One 5½"x 5½" x ¼" (140 x 140 x 6mm) oak board (inlay)
- Two 5½"x 5½" x ½" (140 x 140 x 13mm) oak boards
- Wood glue
- Clamps
- Double-sided tape
- Spray adhesive
- Pencil
- Sharpened putty knife
- Drill and bit
- Band saw
- Sandpaper
- Radial orbit sander (optional)
- Table belt sander (optional)
- Scrap wood
- Wood putty
- Newspaper
- Finish of choice

DESIGN INSPIRATION

This box has a fairly simple, yet effective, design. The pattern is essentially a floral form with each petal overlapping the petal adjacent to it. To give the piece movement, I offset the inner oval of each petal, making a thin side and a thick side to each one. This fills the pattern and hints at motion.

Pattern A

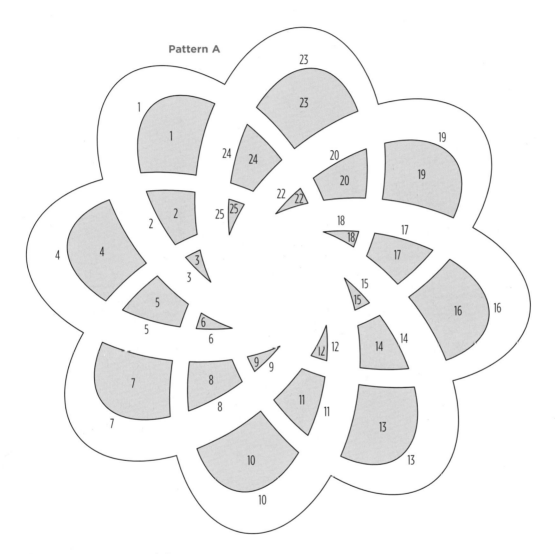

Pattern appears at actual size.

Pattern B

Pattern appears at actual size.

Chinese Lattice

This project can be made using the same process employed for the *Arabian* box (page 105) and has an inlaid lid. Make sure you pay particular attention to the wood grain of the pieces used to make the box. Cut all the boards so the wood grain is running in the same direction, and align the grain of all the pieces before cutting and assembling the box.

DESIGN INSPIRATION

A few years back, I visited an exceptional Chinese garden in Portland, Oregon. I was struck by the complexity of the woodwork throughout the garden, most notably the trellises and window coverings, which had intricate, almost knot-like forms. It occurred to me that these forms would make an attractive scroll saw project. The pattern itself for this project is quite simple—a radial alignment of four squares around a central point with an outer square intersecting the pattern. As with many things, a design does not need to be complex to be beautiful and effective.

TOOLS & MATERIALS

- Three 4½" x 4¼" x ¼" (114 x 114 x 6mm) walnut boards
- One 4½" x 4¼" x ¼" (114 x 114 x 6mm) oak board (inlay)
- Two 5½" x 5½" x ½" (140 x 140 x 13mm) oak boards
- Wood glue
- Clamps
- Double-sided tape
- Spray adhesive
- Drill and bit
- Band saw
- Pencil
- Sharpened putty knife
- Wood putty
- Sandpaper
- Radial orbit sander (optional)
- Table belt sander (optional)
- Newspaper
- Finish of choice

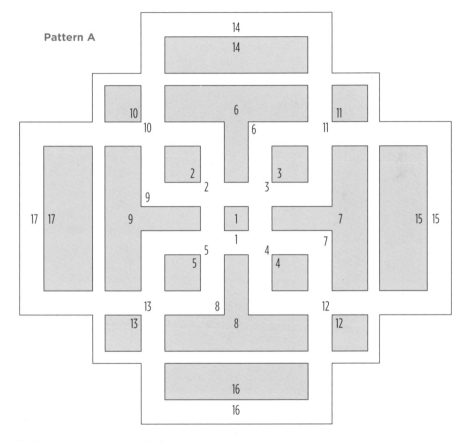

Pattern A

Pattern appears at actual size.

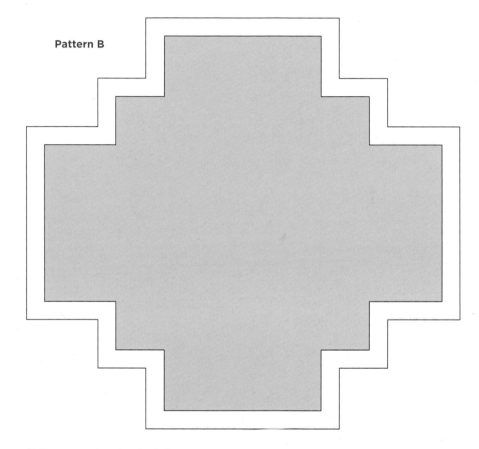

Pattern B

Pattern appears at actual size.

Seed Pods

This project utilizes all of the skills introduced in the book so far and adds one additional component: carving. The rounding of the seedpods attached to the box lid can be done using a rotary tool with a sanding drum attachment. The process for this box might be complicated, but the techniques used to make it are ones you have already employed to complete the previous box projects: thick wood cutting, stack cutting, and inlay.

DESIGN INSPIRATION

Design inspiration can strike you at any moment and come from any unlikely object. The concept for this pattern came to me while I was preparing dinner one night. Cutting open an acorn squash, I was struck by the outside perimeter of undulating lines protecting the seeds inside. While the seeds in the squash were not radially arranged, I chose to arrange them that way in the design, resulting in a much stronger pattern.

TOOLS & MATERIALS

- One 5¾" x 5¾" x ¼" (146 x 146 x 6mm) walnut board (bottom)
- Two 5¾" x 5¾" x ⅛" (146 x 146 x 3mm) walnut boards (top)
- One 5¾" x 5¾" x ⅛" (146 x 146 x 3mm) oak board (top Inlay)
- One 5¾" x 5¾" x ¼" (146 x 146 x 6mm) oak board (top seeds)
- Two 5¾" x 5¾" x ⅝" (146 x 146 x 16mm) oak boards (box body)
- Wood glue
- Clamps
- Double-sided tape
- Spray adhesive
- Pencil
- Sharpened putty knife
- Drill and bit
- Band saw
- Sandpaper
- Rotary tool with drum sander attachment
- Finish of choice

Pattern A

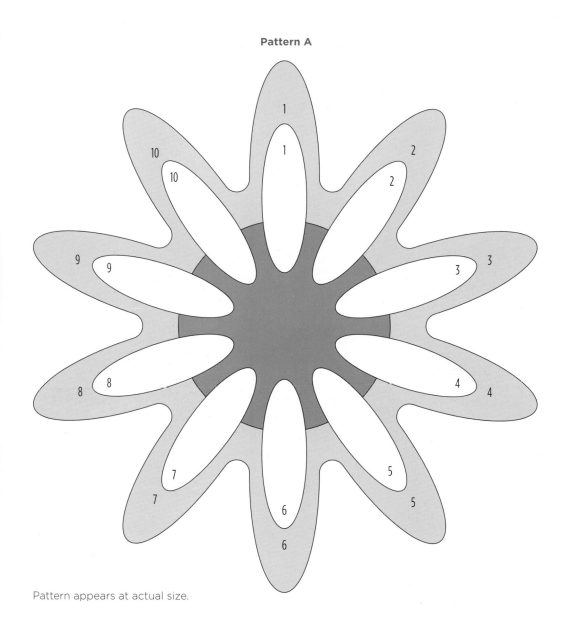

Pattern appears at actual size.

Pattern B

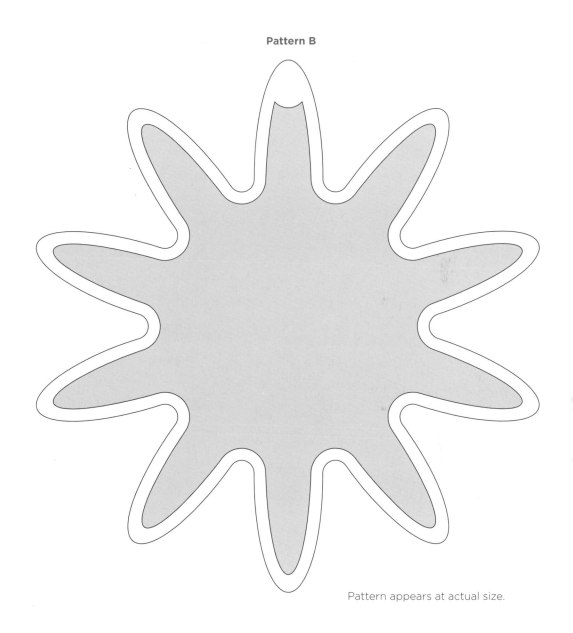

Pattern appears at actual size.

Pattern C

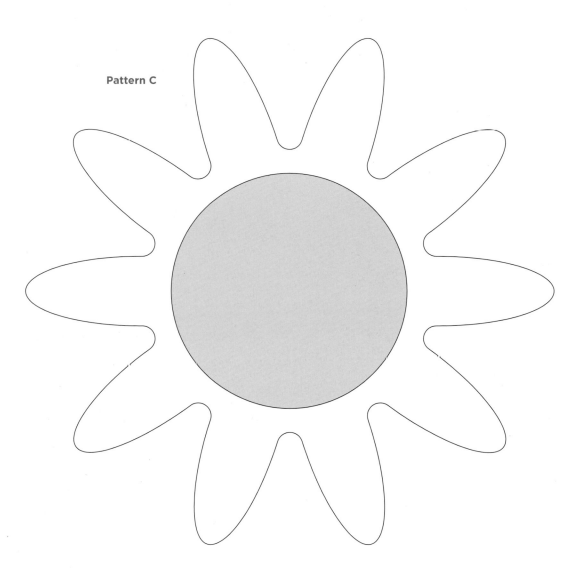

Pattern appears at actual size.

1: CUT THE BOARDS TO SIZE. Cut the wood to the sizes specified in the materials list. Make sure you cut the pieces so the wood grain of all the boards is running in the same direction. Pay careful attention to the wood grain throughout this project, and be sure to align the grain of all the pieces before cutting and assembling the box.

2: MAKE THE BLANK AND ATTACH PATTERN A. To create the box blank, glue the two ⅝" (16mm) oak body pieces together and let dry. Attach the bottom ¼" (6mm) walnut piece to the bottom of the blank with double-sided tape. Tape the two ⅛" (3mm) walnut top pieces together and tape them to the top of the blank. Clamp the blank firmly together and set it aside until the glue has dried. Then, attach Pattern A using spray adhesive.

3: CUT THE OUTSIDE OF THE PATTERN. Cut the outside perimeter of the pattern exactly as you have done for previous projects.

4: MARK THE SIDES. Draw registration marks on the side of the box with a pencil to aid in the final assembly.

5: REMOVE THE TOP AND BOTTOM LAYERS. Using the sharpened putty knife, pry off the top and bottom layers of the box blank and set aside.

6: ATTACH AND CUT PATTERN B. Using spray adhesive, attach Pattern B to the top of the box blank. Drill an access hole and cut out the inside box cavity; set aside.

7: CUT THE LID CATCH. On the band saw, cut a ¼" (6mm)-thick slab from the top of the box cavity waste material from Step 6. Sand both sides of the slab smooth.

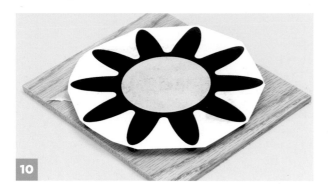

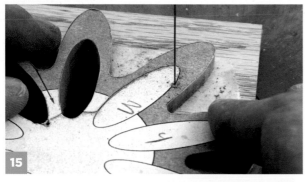

8: SEPARATE THE LID PIECES. Using the sharpened putty knife, gently pry apart the two top walnut pieces that were set aside earlier.

9: ATTACH THE INLAY MATERIAL. Using double-sided tape, attach the walnut piece without a pattern to the top of the ⅛" (3mm) oak inlay material.

10: ATTACH PATTERN C. Using spray adhesive, attach Pattern C to the walnut piece.

11: DRILL AND CUT THE CIRCLE. Drill an access hole through both pieces and carefully cut out the circle from Pattern C.

12: SEPARATE THE LAYERS. Pry the walnut piece and walnut waste material free of the inlay blank. Remove Pattern C from the top of the walnut piece.

13: GLUE THE INLAY. Spread glue carefully on the edges of the oak inlay material. Carefully press it into the walnut lid piece and set it aside to dry.

14: ATTACH THE SEED BOARD. To make the seeds, attach Piece A (the top walnut piece from Step 8) to the ¼" (6mm) oak board for the seeds using double-sided tape. You will use Pattern A as a guide to cut out the seeds.

15: CUT THE SEEDS. Drill an access hole through both pieces and begin to carefully cut out the seeds. You can connect your cuts through the center circle, as this will be removed later. This step is really a variation of the laminate process. Make sure to number the seeds according to the pattern as you cut each one free.

16: CUT THE CENTER CIRCLE. With all the seeds cut free, go back and cut any portion of the inside circle that still remains, removing the waste material.

17: SHAPE THE SEEDS. Using a rotary tool with a sanding drum attachment, gently round the top edges of the seeds. Try not to sand the lower sides of the seeds too much. If they are over sanded, there will be a gap between the seed and the walnut side of the box.

18: GLUE THE LID PIECES. With all of the seeds complete, it is time to reassemble the top of the box. Glue the two walnut top pieces together, using the registration marks on the sides of the pieces to get the correct alignment. For now, leave Pattern A attached to the top piece.

19: MARK THE LID. Write the numbers from Pattern A onto the bottom lid layer. Remove the pattern and sand the top of the lid smooth.

20: GLUE THE SEEDS. Using the numbers, glue the seeds into their correct places on the bottom lid layer and set aside to dry. Remember the numbers should be written on the bottom of the seeds so they don't show when glued. In the image, the seeds have been placed bottom up in the lid with the numbers visible to show how they should be placed.

21: ATTACH THE LID CATCH. When the lid piece is dry, flip it upside down, place the box body on top of it, and align the lid and body using the registration marks. Spread glue evenly over the top of the lid catch. Slide the lid catch through the box body onto the bottom of the box lid. Press firmly to allow the glue to bond, and then carefully remove the box body. Clamp the top and lid catch together firmly and set aside to dry

22: ATTACH THE BOTTOM. Spread glue sparingly onto the bottom of the box body and attach the walnut box bottom, aligning it using the registration marks. Clamp together and set aside to dry.

23: FINISH THE PROJECT. When all the components have dried, remove them from the clamps. Touch up any edges or rough places with sandpaper and erase the registration marks. Finish the box according to your preference.

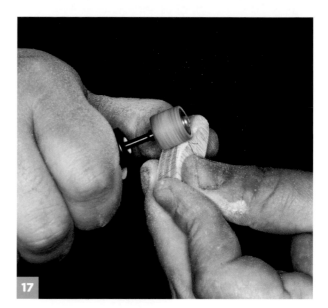

17

20

Rectilinear Spirals

This box is an exploration of the table saw box paired with the scroll saw. For this project, the scroll saw is used to cut tight, inside corners to create the detailed lid of the box.

DESIGN INSPIRATION

The inspiration for this box is a spiral adapted to the confines of the rectangular shape required of any box created on the table saw. Originally, I designed a box with simple flat sides featuring an ornate lid. After completing the box, it occurred to me that the design would be even more attractive if the lines from the top wrapped around the sides of the box, just like the lines on striped wrapping paper wrap around a gift box. I knew lines could be cut into the side of the box with a scroll saw or a band saw.

TOOLS & MATERIALS

- Two 11½" x 2¼" x ¼" (292 x 57 x 6mm) walnut boards (sides—each board makes one long side and one short side of the box)
- One 2½" x 8" x ¼" (64 x 203 x 6mm) walnut board (top)
- One 7½" x 2" x 3⁄16" (191 x 51 x 5mm) cherry board (lid catch)
- One 7¾" x 2¼" x 3⁄16" (197 x 57 x 5mm) cherry board (bottom)
- Table saw
- Miter saw (optional)
- Sandpaper
- Wood glue
- Large rubber bands or band clamps
- Spray adhesive
- Ruler and/or tape measure
- Scrap wood
- Clamps
- Band saw
- Finish of choice

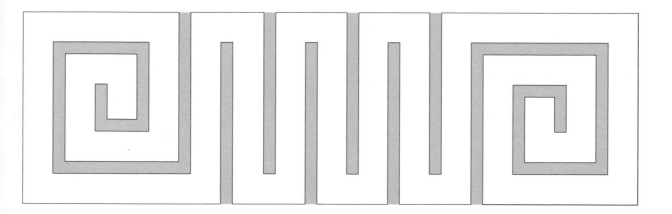

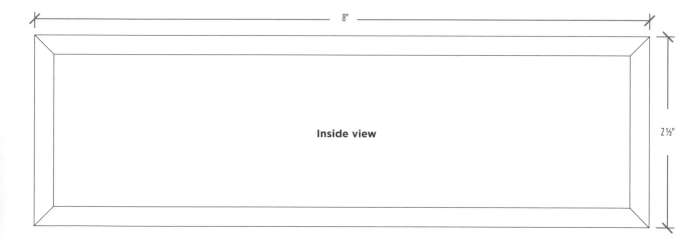

Inside view

8"

2 ½"

Enlarge pattern 125% for actual size.

1: CUT THE BOARDS TO SIZE.

Cut the walnut side boards to the dimensions specified in the materials list. The final outside dimensions of the box are 2 ½" (64mm) wide and 8" (203mm) long. Because shorter pieces are more dangerous to cut, I will combine a short piece with a longer one during milling and cross cut the shorter piece from the board toward the end. Cut the remaining boards to the dimensions specified in the materials list. Make sure you cut the pieces so the wood grain of all the boards is running in the same direction. Pay careful attention to the wood grain throughout this project, and be sure to align the grain of all the pieces before cutting and assembling the box.

2: SET THE SAW.

On the table saw, set the fence 2" (51mm) from the inside edge of the blade. Raise the blade to a little less than ⅛" (3mm).

3: CUT THE GROOVES.

With a side board lying flat, rip cut a ⅛" (3mm)-deep ³⁄₁₆" (5mm)-thick groove ¼" (6mm) from the bottom of the board. Repeat with the second side board. Turn off the saw and set the fence ⁷⁄₁₆" (11mm) from the outside edge of the blade and rip cut the boards again. Turn off the saw and check that the bottom board fits easily into the grooves created in the two side boards. The fit should be slightly loose. The bottom board should be able to float freely in the grooves, so that the box has room to expand and contract with the seasons. Alternatively, you can cut the bottom board from cherry plywood and glue it into the groves of the side boards, as the concerns about wood movement would be eliminated. Gluing in the bottom board strengthens the box by helping to hold the mitered corners together.

4: CUT THE SIDE BOARDS TO THEIR FINAL SIZE AND MITER THE ENDS. Using either a miter saw or the table saw, cut each of the side boards into two pieces, one piece 2½" (64mm) long and one piece 8" (203mm) long. Cut the ends of all four pieces at 45°. Experience has taught me that even with the best digital protractors, this angle will have to be tweaked to create truly airtight joints. For this reason, cut the pieces a little longer at first and test their fit. Make any necessary adjustments to the blade's angle and recut down to the final dimensions.

5: SAND THE BOARDS. Sand the bottom board and the side boards smooth. To avoid rounding the corners, lay a piece of sandpaper on a hard, flat surface and drag the pieces back and forth in the direction of the grain.

6: APPLY GLUE TO THE SIDES. Apply a thin film of glue to all the mitered ends of the side boards. Because the mitered ends are end grain, they tend to absorb some of the glue when it is applied. By putting a thin film of glue on both sides of the mitered joint, there should be enough to create a strong, durable bond.

7: INSERT THE BOTTOM. Before assembling and clamping the box sides, insert the bottom. If you are using solid cherry, do not glue this in place, as it needs to be able to float freely in the grooves. If you have chosen to use cherry plywood, add glue to the grooves in the sideboards and insert the bottom.

8: SECURE THE SIDES. Secure the box together using strong rubber bands. This is an inexpensive way to clamp small boxes. The pressure from the bands will pull on all corners evenly and will ensure a nearly perfect square or rectangular box.

12

9: ATTACH AND CUT PATTERN A. To make the lid, attach Pattern A to the remaining walnut board using spray adhesive. Insert a finish-style blade into the scroll saw (reverse-tooth, crown-tooth, etc.), and begin cutting. Cut one end spiral first, and then move down the board, cutting the notches and finishing with the second spiral. Cutting in this way maintains the strength of the wood for as long as possible during the cut. However, the pieces are still fragile, so use your fingers to give support to the piece as it is cut and rotated. Remove the pattern, and sand any frayed wood that may be left behind.

10: MEASURE AND CUT THE LID CATCH. When the box body has dried, cut the lid catch. I recommend measuring the inside void of the box before cutting. If your measurements were off on the sides, the lid catch listed in the materials list may be the wrong size. When the size is confirmed, cut with the table saw.

11: ATTACH THE LID CATCH. Apply small droplets of glue to the bottom of the lid, and smear this into a thin film. Avoid getting glue within

¼" (6mm) of the edge of the lid, as this portion will be visible in the finished product. Press the lid catch onto the lid (remember to make sure the grain of the lid and lid catch run parallel to one another). Measure to ensure it is ¼" (6mm) from all four edges. Place it between two stiff flat boards and clamp together tightly.

12: CUT THE NOTCHES. When the lid has dried, place it on the box. Install a finish-grade blade in the band saw (typically 32 teeth per inch [25mm]). Check that the table is square. With the saw running, gently push the edge of the box into the blade, aligning the blade with the edges of the notches in the box lid. Chip away at the notches until they are the same width as those in the lid. Note: Cut a little less than a ⅛" (3mm) into the sides of the box. Remember, the bottom of the box is in a ⅛" (3mm) groove and the side of the box is only ¼" (6mm) thick. If you cut ⅛" (3mm) or more into the sides, the bottom of the box may become visible.

13: FINISH THE BOX. When the notches in the box have been completed, touch up any rough spots or excess glue with sandpaper. Finish the box according to your preference.

BUSINESS CARD HOLDERS

In this section, all your knowledge comes into play to take your scroll saw projects beyond the two dimensional pieces normally associated with the scroll saw. These projects build on everything you've learned: thick wood cutting, stack cutting, and, above all, precision. When you work in 3-D with interlocking pieces, each cut must be precisely right or the project won't fit together in the end. The scroll saw is the perfect tool to make the pieces in this section. Since they are all sized to fit a business card, most of the pieces are very small, too small to be safely cut with larger shop equipment.

Business card holders are normally utilitarian items, often little more than a cheap wire holder picked up at an office supply store. But many companies, and artists as well, have their business cards on display in the front of their offices for visitors. By making such a display, you can show your talent and creativity.

60° Repetition

The projects in this section, including this one, use very thin lumber. Because planing short pieces of wood (anything less than 16" [406mm]) can be very dangerous, plane longer pieces of wood before cutting the boards down to the dimensions specified in the materials list. This will leave a lot of extra material that can then be used to make the other business card holder in this section. Since most planers won't plane wood less than ¼" (6mm) in thickness, you may need to build a planing sled (see page 18).

DESIGN INSPIRATION

Repetition is a fundamental design concept, as is graduated sizes. The pattern for this project is based on these two design principles. I knew I wanted a series of vertical planes that grew from thin and short to tall and wide, like an exaggerated perspective of fence posts disappearing to the horizon. From there I toyed with various ways to hold these planes together and incorporate the business cards. After my first model, I realized that a perfectly vertical alignment would cause the cards to fall out, so the design had to be adjusted to slant backward, leaning the cards against the main spine. This real world practical problem forced me to come up with a design solution that was far more aesthetically pleasing than my original concept. This is something to remember should you choose to make your own patterns—design challenges are doorways to new design approaches.

TOOLS & MATERIALS

- One 6" x 4½" x ½" (152 x 114 x 51mm) walnut board (Piece A)
- Two 1 ¹³⁄₁₆" x 1 ¹³⁄₁₆" x ³⁄₁₆" (46 x 46 x 5mm) cherry pieces (Piece B)
- Two 1¼" x 1¼" x ³⁄₁₆" (32 x 32 x 5mm) cherry pieces (Piece C)
- One 4³⁄₁₆" x 1¾" x ³⁄₁₆" (106 x 44 x 5mm) cherry piece (Piece D)
- One 3⅜" x 1⅜" x ³⁄₁₆" (86 x 35 x 5mm) cherry piece (Piece E)
- One 2⅝" x 1" x ³⁄₁₆" (67 x 25 x 5mm) cherry piece (Piece F)
- Miter or table saw
- Spray adhesive
- Masking tape
- Sandpaper
- Table belt sander (optional)
- Wood glue
- Pencil
- Finish of choice

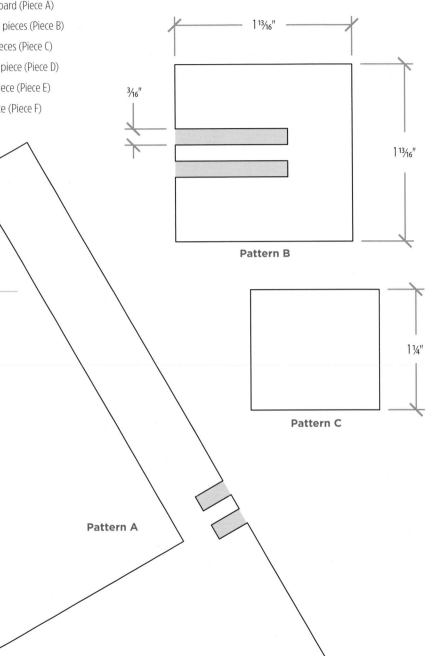

1 ¹³⁄₁₆"

³⁄₁₆"

1 ¹³⁄₁₆"

Pattern B

1 ¼"

Pattern C

Pattern A

Patterns appear
at actual size.

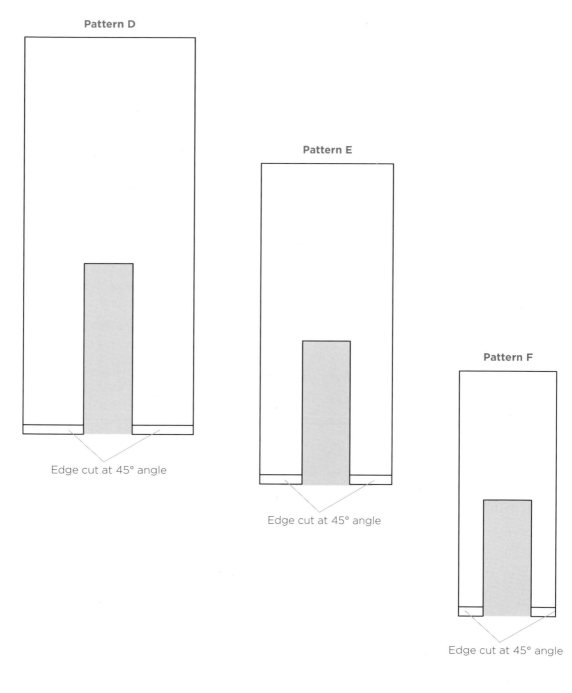

Pattern D

Edge cut at 45° angle

Pattern E

Edge cut at 45° angle

Pattern F

Edge cut at 45° angle

Patterns appear at actual size.

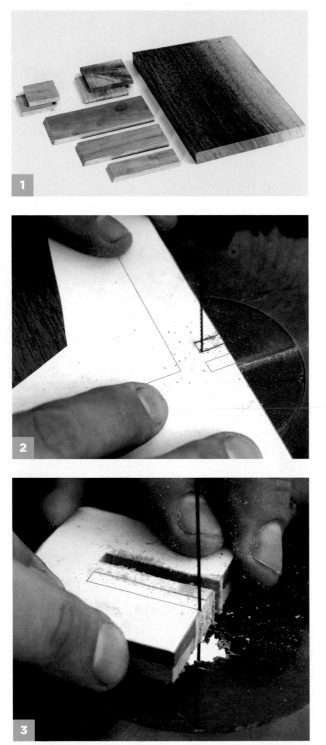

1: CUT THE BOARDS TO SIZE. With the wood planed to the correct thickness, cut the boards to the sizes specified in the materials list. Cut one edge of Pieces D, E, and F at a 45° angle using a miter saw.

2: ATTACH AND CUT PATTERN A. Use spray adhesive to attach Pattern A to its respective piece. Cut the perimeter and the notches of the pattern. The two Piece C boards will be inserted into the notches cut in Piece A, so once the notches are complete, test the fit. The Piece C boards should fit snugly, but not tightly into the notches. If the fit is too tight, lay a C piece over the notch and trace the outline of the piece with a pencil. Carefully recut along the inside of the pencil line. Repeat as necessary to ensure a tight, even fit. Note: The fit should not be loose. Remember, there are still patterns attached. When the patterns are removed and the pieces sanded, they will get a little thinner. If the connection with the pieces is loose now, there will be gaps between later. Recut these pieces if necessary.

3: ATTACH AND CUT PATTERN B. Tape the two pieces of wood for the B pieces together using masking tape. Attach Pattern B and cut out the perimeter and notches. The C pieces will also be inserted into these notches, so test the fit and adjust as in the previous step.

4: ATTACH AND CUT PATTERNS D, E, AND F. Attach Patterns D, E, and F to their respective wood pieces. These pieces will slide over the back of Piece A, so test the fit and adjust as described previously. Note: The pattern for each piece should be placed so the end with the notch is glued to the end of the board with the 45° cut.

5: REMOVE PATTERNS AND SAND. Remove the paper patterns from all the workpieces and the masking tape from the B pieces. Sand all components thoroughly.

6: GLUE PIECES A, B, AND C. Begin to assemble the cardholder using wood glue. Apply a thin film of glue to the notches in the B pieces and insert the C pieces. Apply a thin film of glue to the notches in Piece A and insert the other end of the C pieces. Adjust the pieces until the B pieces are resting firmly against the spine of Piece A and are parallel to each other. Note: You will be gluing some of the pieces together so that the wood grain of one piece is running perpendicular to the grain of another piece. This cannot be avoided, as there is not really another way to cut the pieces for the project. Because the pieces are small and the glue flexible, however, seasonal movement is not a large concern.

7: GLUE PIECE D. Apply a thin film of glue in the notch of Piece D and 2 ¼" (57mm) up from the corner at the back of Piece A. Slide Piece D over the rear leg of Piece A, and press firmly against the spine. Let the pieces dry for about 30 minutes before finishing the assembly.

8: GLUE PIECES E AND F. Pieces E and F will be assembled using a manner similar to that used to attach Piece D. Before installing, mark a line on the rear leg of Piece A that is ⁵⁄₁₆" (8mm) away from the back of Piece D. Apply glue to the notch of Piece E and align the front edge with the pencil mark. Slide Piece E over the rear leg of Piece A. Repeat the process to attach Piece F.

9: SAND THE BOTTOM. When the glue for all the pieces has dried completely, sand the bottom of the cardholder flat. This can be done by laying a sheet of sandpaper on a hard, flat surface and dragging the piece back and forth. You can also use a table belt sander.

10: FINISH THE PROJECT. Check the piece for any rough spots or excess glue and sand smooth. Finish using your preferred method.

Simple Balance

DESIGN INSPIRATION

This project is a simple version of a cardholder. My goal was to showcase cards in this holder in a horizontal position. I wanted the cards to sit on a little platform, like a piece of art. To make the platform appear to float, I wanted a strong shadow line at the base. To do this, I placed a wood piece beneath the platform that was small enough to nearly disappear but large enough to provide stability for the project. The cards also needed some form of side support on the platform to keep them from falling over. I wanted the support to be small enough that it did not cover the whole card, obscuring its information. For the support I chose a simple square that would pierce two vertical planes and hold just the cards' corners. At first, I intended the vertical planes to be solid, but the design evolved so that the cards along with the square would pierce the vertical planes. The final pattern is a simple, clean form, asymmetrically balanced, and relatively simple to build.

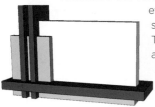

TOOLS & MATERIALS

- One 5" x 2⅛" x ¼" (127 x 54 x 6mm) walnut piece (Piece A)

- Two 3" x 1⅜" x ³⁄₁₆" (76 x 35 x 5mm) walnut pieces (Pieces B and C)

- Two 1⁹⁄₁₆" x 1⁹⁄₁₆" x ⅛" (40 x 40 x 3mm) cherry pieces (Piece D)

- One 4¼" x 1" x 1¼" (108 x 25 x 32mm) walnut piece (Piece E)

- Spray adhesive

- Drill and bit

- Wood glue

- Sandpaper

- Finish of choice

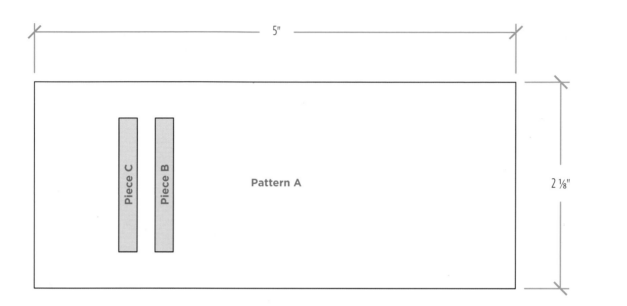

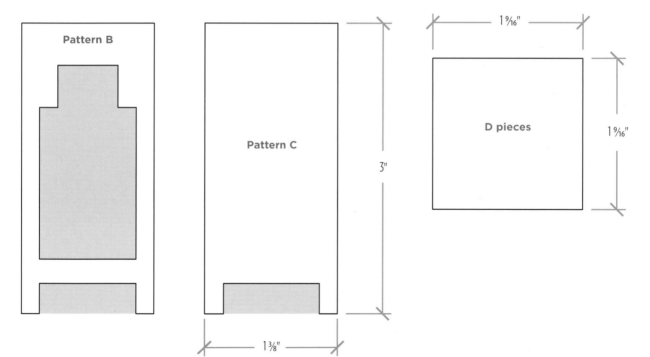

Patterns appear at actual size.

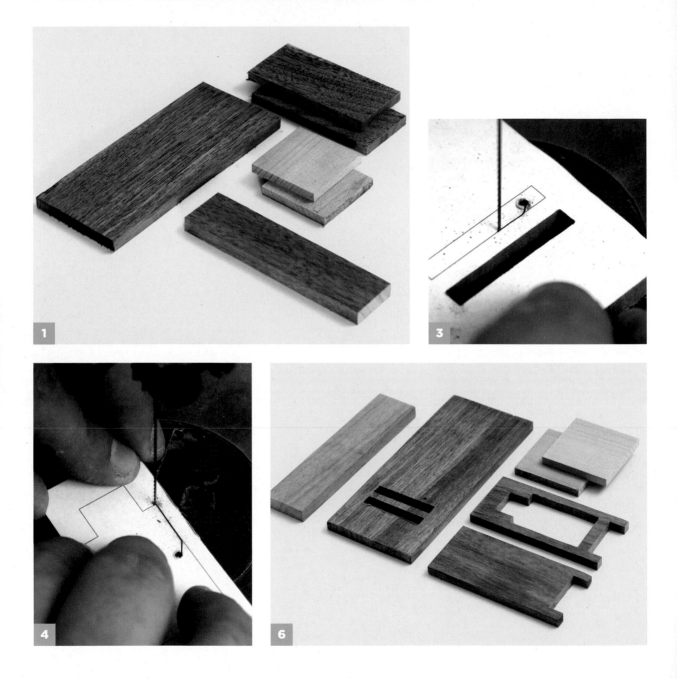

1: CUT THE BOARDS TO SIZE. Cut the wood pieces to the sizes specified in the materials list.

2: ATTACH THE PATTERNS. Attach the patterns to their respective pieces using spray adhesive.

3: DRILL AND CUT PATTERN A. Drill an access hole in Piece A and remove the waste material. Pieces B and C will be inserted into these holes, so test the fit and adjust as necessary.

4: DRILL AND CUT PATTERN B. Drill an access hole in Piece B and cut away the waste material. The two D pieces will be inserted into Piece B, so test the fit and adjust as necessary.

5: CUT PATTERN C. Cut the notch at the bottom of Piece C.

6: REMOVE PATTERNS AND SAND. Remove the paper patterns and sand all the pieces smooth.

7: PLACE PIECES B AND C. Begin assembly by inserting Pieces B and C into Piece A. Pieces B and C will be held in place with the two D pieces, so no glue is required at this stage.

8: GLUE THE D PIECES. Apply a thin film of glue to the inside vertical edge of Piece B and a thin film of glue to the back vertical edge of one of the D pieces. Do not slide the D piece into place, as this would smear the glue. Instead, hold the D piece in the center of Piece B with the rear edge close to Piece C and press into place with the face pressed against Piece B and the back edge pressed against Piece C. Repeat this process for the second D piece on the other side of Piece B. Note: You will be gluing some of the pieces together so that the wood grain of one piece is running perpendicular to the grain of another piece. This cannot be avoided, as there is not really another way to cut the pieces for the project. Because the pieces are small and the glue flexible, however, seasonal movement is not a large concern.

9: GLUE PIECE E. Glue Piece E to the base of the project and let dry.

10: FINISH THE PROJECT. When the glue for all the pieces has dried completely, sand the bottom of the cardholder flat and finish in your preferred method.

INDEX

ACQUISITION EDITOR
Kerri Landis

COPY EDITORS
Paul Hambke and Heather Stauffer

COVER AND LAYOUT DESIGNER
Lindsay Hess

PHOTOGRAPHY
Erin L. Hubbs and Scott Kriner

EDITOR
Katie Weeber

PROOFREADER
Lynda Jo Runkle

INDEXER
Jay Kreider

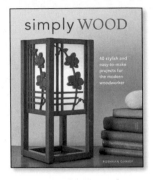

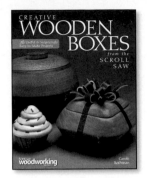
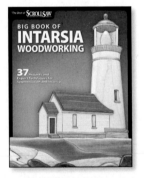
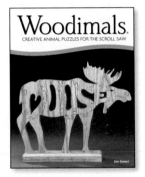